I0459254

LEVERAGING LEADERSHIP

How to Become the Leader That Everyone Wants to Follow

BY LISA KENT

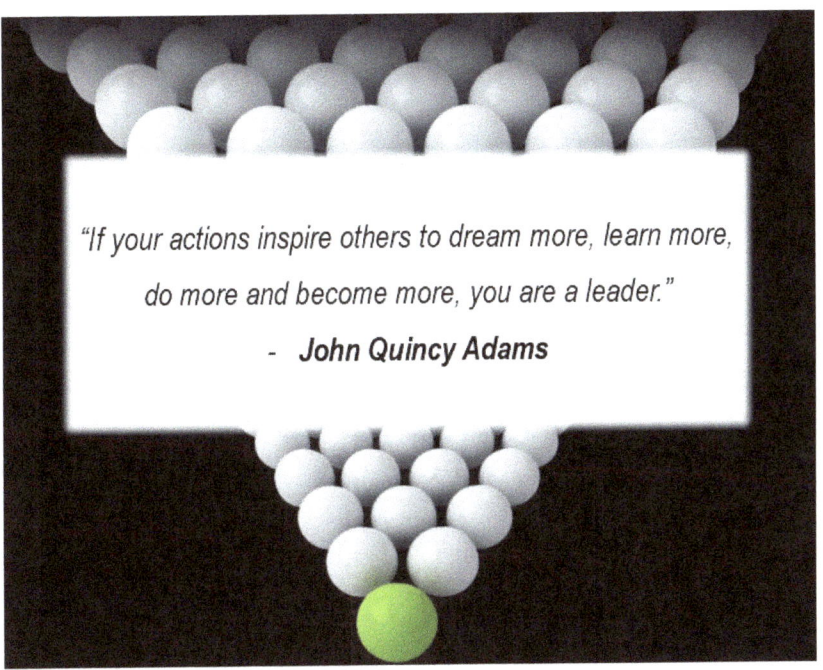

"If your actions inspire others to dream more, learn more, do more and become more, you are a leader."

- John Quincy Adams

TABLE OF CONTENTS

"The challenge of leadership is to be strong, but not rude; be kind, but not weak; be bold, but not bully; be thoughtful, but not lazy; be humble, but not timid; be proud, but not arrogant; have humor, but without folly."

- Jim Rohn, American Author & Motivational Speaker

PREFACE

Business is built on leadership. Any successful endeavor has a history of great, innovative leaders who did what it took to ensure success. They nurtured leadership in others and inspired them to contribute. When studying the history of leadership, one of the first questions that comes to mind is, how do you become the leader that everyone wants to follow?

I have spent a good portion of my life trying to be a better leader. One of the first tenets of leadership is continuous learning – there is always something to learn and something to improve. Yet, in this age of information overload, it can be confusing to know where to go to access leadership learning. For professionals just starting out, acquiring the necessary leadership skills can be a daunting task.

I was lucky because I had access to leadership experiences at an early age. By eighth grade, I was elected to student council and became the editor of the middle school paper. I loved that I could represent my classmates' requests for more dessert options in the cafeteria. I got to document our lives covering all-important dramas like the competition for the best class mural or the new library furniture.

Even back then I knew I wanted to make an impact by leading, or at least guiding and influencing others. In high school, I lost many elections and had to accept club presidencies in lieu of class presidencies. I loved to write and helped immortalize my class' achievements in our yearbook. I became involved in volunteering and realized, for the first time, that service played a pivotal role in leadership. Academics mattered but character, standing up for people, nurturing new ideas, and serving others mattered as well.

Today, as a business leader and teacher, I strive to learn new approaches and to work toward being the best leader I can be. As I have observed so many wonderful (and not so wonderful) leaders during my career, I have developed a sense of what works and what doesn't. No two leaders are alike, but they do have many qualities in common.

I have also worked hard to help engender the leadership qualities I believe are important in my teams over the years and most recently in my marketing firm, Luminations. Through mentoring many young leaders and students, I have realized that it's our job to highlight and reinforce these skills and that it isn't always easy to do.

Today's leaders face many challenges including: an ever-changing workplace, a need for a mastery of big data, a global marketplace, the use of technology in communicating effectively across many different platforms, the know-how to face failures and bounce back fast, and the mission to inspire others through words and action.

I wrote this book for my students, in class and at work, but also for leadership students of any age and at any stage of their careers. I believe that we are all working toward becoming stellar leaders. I wanted to shine a light on the characteristics that really matter in both the evergreen and ever-changing landscape of leadership. My hope is that my personal stories and the thoughtful commentary from so many awesome leaders will showcase those leadership qualities that will help the reader become the leader that everyone wants to follow.

As with my other books, I have been honored and privileged to interview many incredible people and to hear their take on leadership. They share what they have learned from others as well. In almost every case, my request for an interview was welcomed. As busy and in-demand as they were, they all agreed to talk with me. I am incredibly grateful, awed and inspired. One mark of great leaders is that they are selfless in wanting to share their learning. They were gracious in offering their time and lessons and I want to send a special thank you to: Alissa Hsu-Lynch, Bill McComb, Carla Vernón, Karen Connelly, Sharon D'Agostino, Sheri McCoy, Owen Rankin, Jason Barnett, Mari Baker, Wendy Van Besien, Tom Weck, and Sacha Connor.

Through their eyes and mine, I hope you will get a sense of the key ingredients of strong leadership and some easy tips on how to get there. While some concepts are not new, in fact they are tried and true, they come with real life examples and answers, to "what do I do now?" As always, I welcome your feedback and thoughts and look forward to seeing you as the amazing leader I know you will become (if you're not there already).

LEARNING FROM HISTORY

*Defining Leadership Past,
Present and Future*

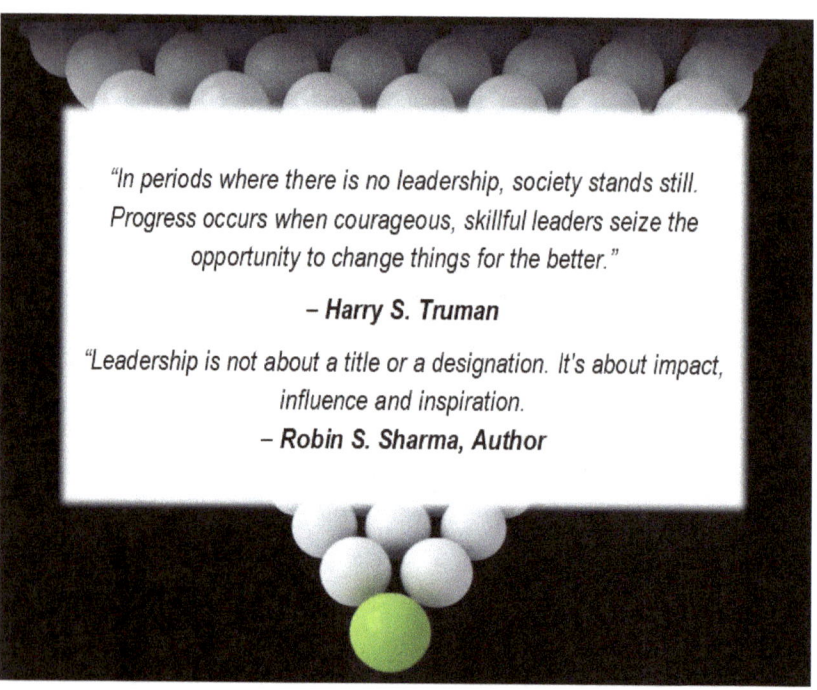

"In periods where there is no leadership, society stands still. Progress occurs when courageous, skillful leaders seize the opportunity to change things for the better."

– Harry S. Truman

"Leadership is not about a title or a designation. It's about impact, influence and inspiration.

– Robin S. Sharma, Author

LEARNING FROM HISTORY
Defining Leadership Past, Present and Future

Leadership is an undisputed essential fundamental of successful business. However, leadership is a complex concept - more complex than we may think at first glance. Just a simple Google search on top leadership skills produces thousands of results, and all this information can be overwhelming.

When trying to determine what makes a great leader, the first thing to consider is perspective. Many versions of this story have been told over the years, but I really like how Jay Shetty, a current trending speaker, told it in a video recently.

A young executive was at an airport about to board his flight when it was announced that there was going to be a three-hour delay before taking off. He was annoyed but knew there was nothing he could do about it.

So, the young executive went to a coffee shop and decided to get a box of six cookies. He sat down, took out a book and settled in to read and eat his cookies. Soon after, another man sat down across the table from him. They briefly locked eyes, but as the young executive was entrenched in his book, he dropped his eyes back to the page in front of him as he reached out and took a cookie. To his surprise, he soon heard a rustle of plastic and noticed the man across from him was taking a cookie.

The executive could not believe how bold this other guy was – just taking a cookie without asking. Fuming, he took another cookie and went back to reading his book. Soon, there was only one cookie left and the other man picked it up, broke it in half and offered it to the executive.

Angrily, the executive took the offered half of a cookie, glaring at the man opposite him but still saying nothing. Soon after, the man on the other side of the table got up and left the coffee shop. Still silently fuming about the audacity of the guy who had eaten his cookies without asking, the executive decided to head toward his gate. He leaned down and picked up his briefcase, only to be confronted by his unopened box of six cookies.

Realization struck him. He had been eating the other man's cookies! He then realized that all his negative energy had been for nothing. He had made a series of incorrect assumptions based on his point of view. He believed that the other man was eating his cookies – and he based all his thoughts and actions on this incorrect assumption.

Once his point of view changed, he realized he had been the interloper, the one stealing cookies without asking. Perspective changed everything.

Getting the Right Perspective

So how do we get the right perspective on leadership? The best way to begin is to have a quick look at history. Traditionally, leadership has been very patriarchal, totally controlled by the males in society with limited exception over the years.

One of those exceptions was Cleopatra, Queen of Egypt. History sees her as a strong leader, one who led at a time when Egypt was besieged by Rome and terrible famine starved her people. Yet she still had to fight against the stereotypical male leaders in the form of her own brothers.

Many historians remember her more for her feminine wiles and her royal birth. However, she should also be immortalized as a strong, diplomatic leader with skills that were debatably better than the men's leadership skills of that era. She understood strategy and the need to make sacrifices in order to put the good of her subjects ahead of her own personal wants. She not only resurrected many ancient traditions that had been lost, she pushed on to create a booming economy and gathered information for the library at Alexandria. We need to remember her as a strong, confident leader who influenced her people, Egypt, and eventually the entire world.

The Context of Leadership

Fast forward a few millennia to the 20th century and the story of Winston Churchill, which presents some interesting questions and answers on the subject of leadership. One of Winston Churchill's chief attributes as a leader was his ability to inspire people, despite ominous circumstances. The source of this inspiration was his own character. Churchill's public persona demonstrated enthusiasm, determination, and optimism. Others jumped to assist.

One of Churchill's private secretaries spoke of Churchill's impact, "Government departments, which under Neville Chamberlain, had continued to work at much the same speed as in peacetime, awoke to the realities of war. They wanted to impress Churchill. A sense of urgency was created in the course of very few days and respectable civil servants were actually to be seen running along the corridors. No delays were condoned; telephone switchboards quadrupled their efficiency; the Chiefs of Staff and the Joint Planning Staff were in almost constant session; regular office hours ceased to exist and weekends disappeared with them."

Churchill's ability to inspire and become the leader everyone wanted to follow was necessary in the opening days of World War II. He did not permit a defeatist attitude, nor would he entertain talk of negotiated terms with Adolf Hitler.

As his official biographer, Sir Martin Gilbert wrote, "It was Churchill's own opposition to all forms of defeatism that marked out the first six months of his war premiership and established the nature and pattern of his war leadership."

Another example of Churchill's power of inspiration was his ability to channel his determination to all the British people. He strengthened their resolve through enthusiastic encouragement and praise of others. Churchill inspired not only British leaders, but British citizens as well, by projecting an attitude of optimism and fortitude despite the knowledge that his military forces might not be ready.

Churchill's robust optimism is showcased in a speech he made in the House of Commons on June 4, 1940, when he spoke these famous, often quoted words:

"We shall go on to the end. We shall fight in France, we shall fight on the seas and oceans, we shall fight with growing confidence and growing strength in the air, we shall defend our island, whatever the cost may be. We shall fight on beaches, we shall fight on the landing grounds, we shall fight in the fields and in the streets, we shall fight in the hills; we shall never surrender."

Beyond his ability to motivate and communicate, Winston Churchill was effective because he had strategic foresight. He sensed what people needed and then delivered it. There was another factor that elevated all his talents: his passion. Winston Churchill possessed a passion for democratic freedom that drove him to work hard for its preservation and bring thousands along with him. He was an effective statesman and leader, one that most of Great Britain wanted to follow.

In 1945, six years after the Second World War began, peace was declared in Britain. Britain's Prime Minister had faithfully led Britain through the war to victory.

David Dilks, author of *Sir Winston Churchill*, believes that "Churchill, although an incomparable leader in war, was too aggressive for times of peace."

Churchill's passion for the conduct of war and military victory was certainly one of his most important goals. Everything else, including party politics, came in second. So, when the war came to an end, Churchill found himself without a clear sense of purpose or direction.

Though a successful wartime leader, Winston Churchill never achieved the same success in peacetime. His personality did not reflect the calm and passive spirit expected in a peacetime leader. He was a constant reminder of war. No one can deny however, that he was a great man. It can be said that he was the reason for peace, though he could not adapt easily.

In Churchill's own words: "Success is not final, failure is not fatal: it is the courage to continue that counts." His success as a leader needed the context of war, and when it came to peace, without a shift in approach and clear vision, few wanted to follow him. A different perspective needed a different approach.

Feminine Framework

In the U.S. at the same time as Churchill was inspiring the British, both Roosevelts were inspiring Americans. Eleanor took on a brave role as her husband led the country. She said, "The future belongs to those who believe in the beauty of their dreams."

As the wife of Franklin D. Roosevelt, the 32nd President of the United States, Eleanor Roosevelt helped redefine the role of the First Lady. Eleanor not only participated in radio broadcasts, she also authored a daily syndicated column, held press conferences to discuss women's issues and was an active supporter of civil rights policies and New Deal social welfare programs.

She transformed what had been a ceremonial role into a real position. On his first day as president, Franklin Roosevelt announced that he was going to have a press conference. Eleanor decided to hold her own press conference that same day, but she made a rule that only female reporters could come.

This meant that, all over the country, publishers had to hire their first female reporters if they wanted to be able to report on the First Lady's issues. An entire generation of female journalists got their start because of her. She became an early leader of the feminist movement while still acting as a partner, with quiet determination. She also traveled 200 days a year. She would talk to constituents and bring back anecdotes and stories. In essence, she was a curious investigative First Lady who offered an outside understanding to the administration.

After President Roosevelt's death, Eleanor continued her humanitarian efforts by helping to develop the Universal Declaration of Human Rights and UNICEF. Her ability to redefine expectations is a reminder that great leaders always look for opportunities to break the mold and pull others along with them.

Leadership Characteristics

Of course, leadership is not just about being a person who is admired by history, though that can be part of it. It's also about being the person who can drive a team to achieve results. It's inspiring people to achieve more, to work to their fullest potential. Leadership is also teaching, coaching and cheerleading. Leadership is ensuring that problems are solved or at least offering the tools to solve them. It is about steering the ship and setting the goals and then making sure they're accomplished.

By comparing many experts' ideas and talking to dozens of outstanding leaders, I have developed a summary of the characteristics that I believe are important leadership considerations. They can help anyone become the leader that everyone wants to follow:

- Have a sense of **ethics** and tell the truth

- Offer both **passion** and **purpose**

- Really **care** about the individuals we lead

- Build a team of **experts**, don't be intimidated by them and most of all, know how to delegate

- Effectively **communicate** at all levels – storytelling with a sense of humor is a must

- Admit what we don't know and have **insatiable curiosity** and **resilience**

- Show true grit and **total commitment;** have the **courage** to take risks and the guts to take responsibility for failures

- Lead with a **positive attitude**; optimism is contagious

- Last, but certainly not least, always **inspire** others and **celebrate** their wins. Leadership isn't really about us but about those we will lead

My Path to Leadership

Like many people, my first introduction to leadership was in observing my parents. My mom was a great innovator who decided to create her own business as a way to generate an income while looking after her family.

My mom was working, going to school and taking care of three kids when she saw a need nobody seemed to be addressing. There was a demand for babysitting services when parents wanted to get away without their kids. This was back in the day when it was traditional for married couples to vacation together and leave their kids at home. Not everyone had local grandparents who could step in.

My mom realized that the graduate students at her local university needed income and were generally trustworthy. She began matching graduate student couples to babysit for young families who wanted to escape on a vacation. It was pretty novel at the time and it began to expand to other universities. She found both the vacationers and hired the sitters. She checked everyone out thoroughly, often trying new sitters out on us first. As the guinea pigs, we pressure tested many grad students. She kept only the best. She built her team of sitters and a thriving recurring business from home. Her astute observations, passion, and creativity were apparent (although I'm sure I never acknowledged them back then).

I learned that leadership meant not just having the passion for an idea but also having the courage to take a risk to try it. Good leadership practice also meant surrounding herself with top talent.

My first observation of leadership in the outside business world came when I got my earliest job at the age of 16. I lived in a pretty residential area and had to be able to get to work on my own. There really were not a lot of choices.

However, there was a Sears warehouse about a mile from my house. If you didn't drive a forklift, you had only two options in terms of job choice. You could work in the parts department fulfilling orders for appliance repairs, or you could work in the maintenance agreement department, which was cold calling telephone sales.

I chose the latter because I was not afraid to talk. Most importantly, the job did not begin until 5:30 at night (you may remember sales phone calls during the dinner hour), and that fit with my schedule of school and sports.

At age 16, I was the youngest person there. Most of the other telephone sales representatives were 30 or older and had been doing this for quite some time.

Our manager, Donna Boucher, had to onboard, nurture and support everyone. She demonstrated outstanding leadership skills and she inspired a lot of confidence in the people she led.

Despite my never having sold anything, Donna made me believe I could do this. The only training was on a cassette tape. We listened to the script and then we started out selling service agreements on lower-end garage door openers, as the cost for their simple maintenance agreements was only $10 per year.

When I made my first sale, she made a celebration out of it. Donna would stop everyone, have them get off their phones and get up to clap and cheer. She would do this again when we made our first sale at the next level, and so on. She always found a reason to celebrate little milestones and acknowledge success. Recognition, verbal not just monetary, was her motto. This was motivating as Sears offered limited commissions.

I learned, at an early age, that quality leaders always find things to celebrate. They encourage and they don't feel threatened by the success of their team. I also learned that she truly believed we could accomplish big things, so her dreams and confidence became ours.

How to Become the Leader Everyone Wants to Follow

There is no magic pill or pivotal moment when someone says "oh, I'm a leader now." Becoming a leader is a work in progress over time, and it is important to know and understand all the elements that go into the process of becoming a good leader before undertaking that journey.

In the following chapters, we will explore the various levels of leadership and hear from industry leaders on what aspects they believe are most important for true and lasting leadership development. In writing this book, I have had the privilege of interviewing so many of the leaders who inspire me. One of the things I have identified is that we are all seeing a profound shift in what defines stellar leadership today. Never before has resilience, failing fast, flexibility, curiosity, and emotional intelligence mattered more.

It is my sincere wish that by sharing my stories, and the stories of others, I can help readers forge a path for themselves to become the kind of leader that everyone wants to follow.

Leveraging Leadership Concepts – So What Now?

1. Putting things in perspective is a great first step in leadership development: Be sure you are looking at situations from multiple angles before acting. Think of the box of cookies.

2. Learn from history: Read at least two books about great leaders in the next 6 months.

3. Recognize that becoming a great leader is a process: Set short-term goals for yourself and check them off as you achieve them.

THE ETHICS OF LEADERSHIP

Trust, Truth and Authenticity

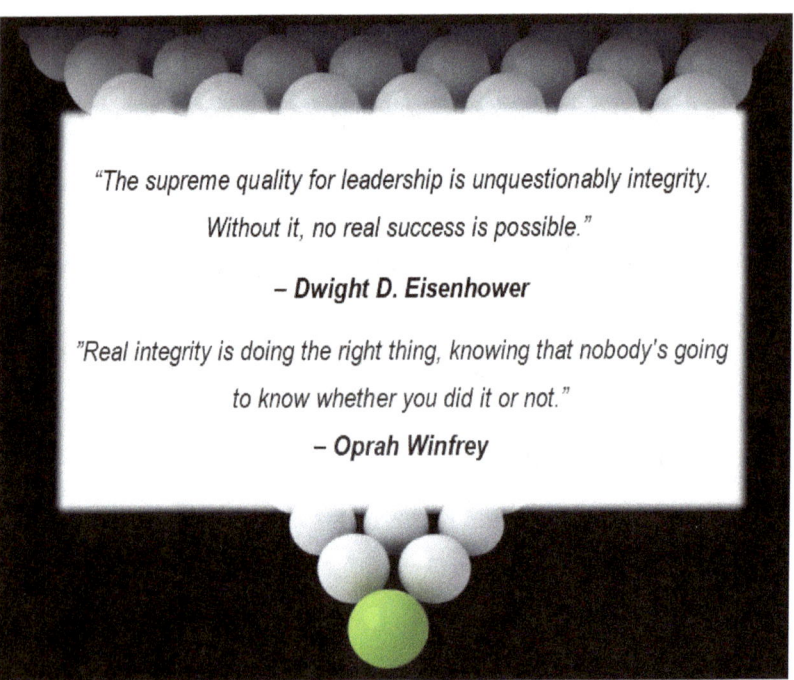

"The supreme quality for leadership is unquestionably integrity. Without it, no real success is possible."

– Dwight D. Eisenhower

"Real integrity is doing the right thing, knowing that nobody's going to know whether you did it or not."

– Oprah Winfrey

THE ETHICS OF LEADERSHIP

Trust, Truth and Authenticity

W e can't really discuss ethical leadership without looking first at ethics as a concept. We could ask 100 different people what they think ethics are and would probably get 100 different answers.

This struggle to define ethics can be traced back to prehistoric times, where the questions and concepts served as a cornerstone for both ancient Greek Philosophy and many major world religions.

Growing up, the concept of ethics was simple for me. I followed the golden rule of do unto others, as you'd have them do unto you. I tried to do what I believed was right at all times.

As I got older, knowing exactly what was right became harder to define. I had to trust my instincts even when the world seemed filled with gray areas.

In most business decisions, ethics are based on a set of social norms in the broader context of morality. However, ethics can be open to interpretation in many ways, as detailed in an article by Community Tool Box. The article defines ethics in many diverse ways and it's worth at least considering his spectrum as we approach decisions.

Situational ethics mean what's right could depend on the context of the situation. What's right in one situation may be wrong in another.

Culturally-relative ethics mean that whatever a culture deems right is ethical for that culture and may differ from our own.

Professional ethics mean many professions including law, medicine, and psychotherapy have their own specific codes of ethics which all members of those professions are expected to follow. Members of those professions are considered ethical in their practice if they adhere to the code of their profession.

Rule-based ethics mean that if we follow the rules (of our company, organization, peer group, culture, or religion) then we are behaving ethically.

I also often think about Villanova University's 4-V model of ethical leadership. This model aligns internal beliefs and values with external ones, for the common good. The 4 V's stand for Values, Vision, Voice and Virtue.

Their study concluded that the main goal of an ethical leader is to create a world in which the future is positive and inclusive, and an ethical leader must foster these goals to succeed. This also allows for the potential of each individual to grow and meet his/her highest potential.

Levels of Ethical Leadership

Ethical leaders can help establish a positive environment with productive relationships at three levels: the individual, the team and the entire organization. By carefully nurturing relationships at each of these levels, a true leader can produce results and nurture talent.

First: The Well-Being of the Individual

Maintaining a positive working atmosphere is an important responsibility of the strong ethical leader. One who leads by example can influence others to do the same. In simple terms, people are affected by the interactions that occur around them. Lots of tension and negative interactions can be a disincentive, while positive communication may help influence job productivity and attitude. Practicing the golden rule works, but it must be seen as the authentic habit of the leader, not just something that she or he does to appear positive.

Second: The Energy of the Team

Ethical leadership can also involve the management of conduct and collaboration within a team. Typically, morale is higher in the workplace when people are getting along with each other and do not take credit for each other's work. When co-workers are working as a cohesive team, it can ensure that the overall performance of the group is at its highest potential. Good leaders lead by example and find positive ways to support a team in accomplishing goals. I was recently reading about heroes as Apollo 11 experienced its 50th anniversary. Most leaders who are classified as heroes recognize the collaborative effort of the team vs. taking solo credit for themselves. The Apollo 11 astronauts did this and quotes from several pilots who successfully landed disabled planes in the past mirror the sentiment. Capt. Sullenberger who successfully navigated a Hudson River crash of his US Air flight, preventing any serious injuries, humbly said, "We were simply doing the jobs we were paid to do." United Airlines Pilot Al Haynes, of a flight that crashed in Sioux City, Iowa said, "There is just a group of four people who did their job."

Third: The Health of the Organization

The importance of maintaining a positive attitude in the workplace has a lot to do with improving the overall health of the organization. When people can show respect for one another, and can value other opinions, it may help create a productive working environment. An ethical organization grows out of an environment of mutual respect, where individuals can grow personally, build friendships and all contribute to a clearly-defined overall mission. Strong leaders articulate the mission, built around ethics, and keep the organization honest.

The world has gotten so competitive that it is common to see people do whatever it takes to be the best. Ethics are often pushed aside. This can become a murky area if the ethical path isn't clearly defined. As we've seen, this can land a company and its leadership in hot water.

When a company or its leaders don't adhere to a moral code, then unethical actions are almost inevitable. Once this downward spiral begins, it is extremely hard to recover. While it is important for leaders to make sure that a company or organization operates ethically, it can get tricky to navigate the day-to-day specifics to ensure an ethical organization.

The *Forbes Coaches Council* recently published an article that outlined practical tips that help keep ethics at the forefront of leadership. They recommended steps that force us to check against our own judgment, as follows:

1. **Perform Simple Tests:** I've seen the impact of working for a leader who said: "Do the right thing, even when no one is looking." I've also seen the impact of working for one who didn't care about ethics.

   Here are two simple tests to gauge what's right: 1 - How would you feel if what you did was printed in your hometown newspaper and your mom read it? 2 - If it related to an employee, how would you feel if your adult child came home and told you she was treated this way at work? *(Kathy Bernhard, KFB Leadership Solutions)*

2. **Focus On Your Daily Decisions:** It takes many years of training to make it to the Olympics. The athletes who try to shortcut the process never make it. If your goals are your numbers for this month only, it's hard to think long-term and easier to be tempted to take shortcuts. Focus on two to five longer-term goals and your day-to-day decisions will be solid, ethical decisions that will help you win your professional Olympics. *(Ruben Gonzales, Olympian Motivation)*

3. **Make Sure You Can Sleep Easily:** How well are you sleeping at night? If you are losing sleep over some of the decisions you are making, you might not be living out your values. Your body and emotions know when you are doing something wrong. Follow the impulses that are guiding you and you will stay on the right, ethical path. *(Monica Thakrar, MTI)*

4. **Express Your Morals:** Your morals are innate and intuitive. Thinking either of those happens passively is a huge mistake. Things become second nature only through habit. How consistent are you in stating what they are? When's the last time you wrote them down? If you're not intentional, then you're not following your compass. *(Derrick Bass, Clarity Provoked)*

5. **Remember Why You Started:** It helps me to stay focused on the customer, to remember I started this company to help people, and to put the human beings who purchase from me above everything else. *(Amanda Frances, Inc.)*

How to Make Telling the Truth Work for You

Early in my career at Johnson and Johnson, I found myself in an interesting leadership position that posed a great ethical question. I worked on a very big ($300 MM) brand where four items in the line represented probably half of our revenue, so we are talking around $150 million worth of business.

The plant that efficiently manufactured these items was in Puerto Rico. The tax laws changed in the U.S. and the company decided to move manufacturing and filling back to America, to a plant that had never manufactured this type of product.

Before I took over this particular business, the prior supply chain team had built the inventory they thought was needed to buffer this relocation. They filled our distribution centers with an extra 120 days of supply and began breaking down and transferring the equipment from Puerto Rico to the U.S.

We had to create a plan for migrating manufacturing plants back to the U.S. We also had to build a complex cross-functional team in order to accomplish this major feat. It was my responsibility to lead the team that would interface with our retailers and our customers to make sure they were happy.

We began manufacturing in the U.S. to start making the products and tested them to ensure they met all expectations and there were no variations in quality. We tried to ensure that the change would be seamless to the consumer. All of this should have been done prior to shutting down the manufacturing plants in Puerto Rico.

In the new U.S. location, the plant team assembled the equipment, and lo and behold, they couldn't get it to work. The U.S. did not have expertise in this type of manufacturing, so it took much longer than they had thought to set up the lines. They had not brought the experts from Puerto Rico to teach them and they believed they had plenty of inventory, but they did not. As plans were made to fix and restart the new line, the pre-built inventory was rapidly depleted.

Some of our largest customers began complaining - Walmart, Kmart and Target. We put together a crisis team that was led by an operations manager, Tom Weck, for whom I have infinite respect. He was, fortunately, ex-military. His VUCA (volatility, uncertainty, complexity, ambiguity) experience helped us a lot. We had to figure out a plan with our remaining inventory. How were we going to allocate it and let our customers know what they were and were not going to get - and still preserve our market share?

Then, we asked ourselves, "how are we going to get ourselves out of this hole with manufacturing?" Tom put together an outstanding plan. We talked it through because I was in charge of the brand and it was up to me to communicate to our team and customers. It was optimistic, or you could argue a little crazy. It required our communicating an apology to our consumers and retailers, to try to maintain their loyalty, while we outlined how we were going to fix the problem by getting manufacturing up and running again.

We had no choice but to be optimistic. We went in with extreme confidence and told each team member what he/she was responsible for and by when we expected the result. The team knuckled down and worked their proverbial butts off, and they were ultimately successful. The level of confidence and the clarity with which Tom articulated the plan was key to making it work.

Our demands were aggressive. First, pull in the experts we needed to get the line up and running in the U.S. fast. Second, build inventory quickly once the line was running at 3 shifts, 7 days, whatever it took. Third, allocate remaining product carefully across priority retailers. Fourth, candidly let consumers know of our regrets and timeline to resolution. Finally, incentivize them to stay with the brand.

Communicating this plan clearly, honestly, and confidently to all constituents was critical. Not everyone at the company supported our coming out and telling the truth. There were management fears that our customers would ridicule our lack of business judgment and other fears about losing our shelf space.

However, I felt strongly that consumers needed to know to hang on to await their beloved product. Retailers needed to know revenue losses were short-lived, and the internal company team needed to know that the extra effort was imperative and that their effort was valued. I might have been running the brand, but appointing a strong, respected leader and sharing communication with him was one of the smartest things I did. The specific action plan, communicated clearly in a confident style, urged an overwhelmed and anxious team on to success. Today, Tom will also say he was able to act as a formidable leader partly because he felt valued and his expertise was trusted.

So, it was my job, as the leader, to explain this difficult situation to our individual customers/retailers. I was truthful with them about what had happened, what the current situation was and what the projected timeline looked like for getting back to normal.

Like George Bailey in the bank scene in *It's a Wonderful Life*, I asked them each what they could get by with in terms of product supply, so that we could make sure everyone would at least receive some inventory.

We also had to launch a campaign to tell consumers what was going on and we apologized and asked them to bear with us. By being totally truthful, we gained the trust of our consumers and they stayed with us. In fact, we even eventually gained market share. The company's fear about the competition taking share was never realized.

Tom gets most of the credit. He put a killer plan in place to get us back on track. While I was managing the communication, he was managing the logistics. Because I knew I had a great co-leader and such a terrific team, I could go out and tell the truth about the situation and know that my team had my back.

Two-way trust was imperative. By entrusting the team and their skills we moved quickly. By doing what we committed to do and finding a solution, we built trust in our leadership approach. Leaders have to tell the truth, do what they promise to do, and act with honesty. In the TV show *Stranger Things*, Elle reminds the group repeatedly "friends don't lie." I agree, don't lie. Earning legitimate trust should always be our goal.

Are You a Leader or a Boss?

There is an evident difference between a leader and a boss, and the way they make others feel. Do they abuse their power to intimidate workers, or do they lead by example? Trust counts and leading by example is key to managing a healthy, happy team.

"In today's transparent social-media-driven world, senior executives, especially those with a high profile, will be tested and called to task over their morals and ethics in how they do business," said Shane Green, author of Culture Hacker. "Businesses and their leaders are under a microscope. How they act and interact with those around them professionally will have a significant impact on their ability to attract new talent and ultimately their bottom lines."

Ethics and kindness should be the go-to approach, even if not publicly acknowledged as the best leadership track to follow. However, now more than ever, deviating from this approach defines you as a boss instead of an ethical leader. Every person in a management position should show ethical leadership. This style of leading fosters an environment of trust and respect.

Define and Align Your Morals

Consider the values you had growing up – treat others how you want to be treated, always say "thank you," and offer support to those who are struggling. As you grow, and as society progresses, conventions can change, often causing values to shift. Be sure your values shift intentionally.

Ask yourself what matters to you as an individual and then align that with your priorities as a leader. Defining your own morals not only expresses your authenticity, it encourages your team to do the same, creating a shared vision for the organization. Build a team whose ethics align and then hire and develop those who share those ethics.

"I do not believe that every person is a fit for every company, and that is okay," said Green. "Companies need to do a better job ensuring they find people who are aligned with their values rather than just hiring for experience." In fact, Green believes it's valuable to hire employees who have different experiences and perspectives because they each offer their own solutions to challenges. I agree and this has been my practice for decades. Seek diverse thinking and diverse backgrounds but common values.

"Nobody wants to work for somebody who doesn't share their values… Without mutual respect, it is very difficult to form a dynamic team, and most people find it very difficult to respect someone who doesn't share their values," says Green.

Ethical leadership, confidence, mutual trust and open, transparent communication are key elements of success, when you want to become the leader that everyone wants to follow.

Leveraging Leadership Concepts - So What Now?

1. Define your own values: make a list and keep it close; check your decisions against it.

2. Your team will follow you anywhere if they trust you. Seek opportunities to build trust by supporting others' perspectives and decisions publicly. Do what you promise to do.

3. Honesty really is the best policy: if you aren't being totally truthful in your interactions, start now.

4. Act like a leader and it won't matter if you're officially the boss. Try it with your team in your next 3 meetings and watch the results.

PASSION WITH PURPOSE

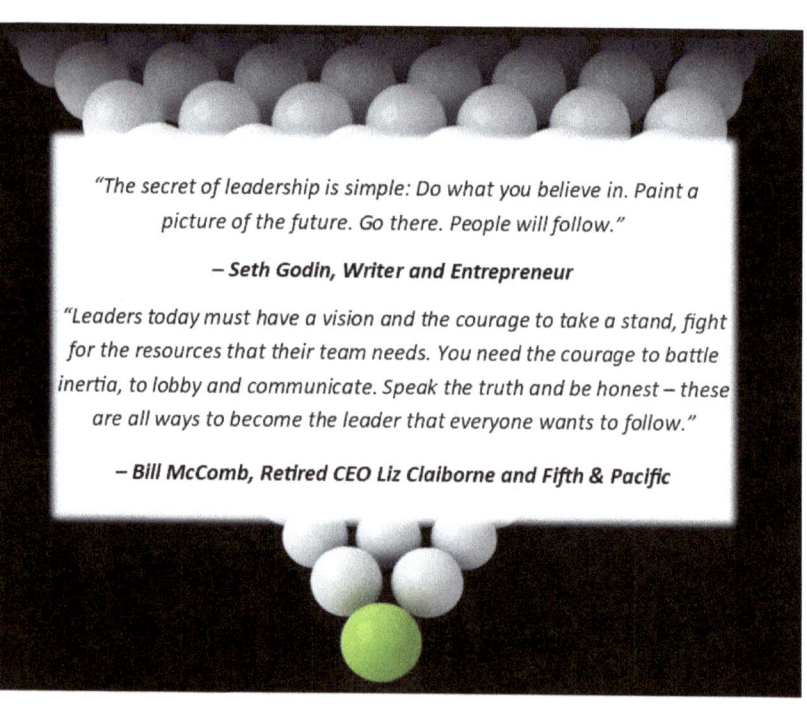

"The secret of leadership is simple: Do what you believe in. Paint a picture of the future. Go there. People will follow."

— Seth Godin, Writer and Entrepreneur

"Leaders today must have a vision and the courage to take a stand, fight for the resources that their team needs. You need the courage to battle inertia, to lobby and communicate. Speak the truth and be honest – these are all ways to become the leader that everyone wants to follow."

— Bill McComb, Retired CEO Liz Claiborne and Fifth & Pacific

PASSION WITH PURPOSE

A s leadership expert Warren Bennis once stated, "Leadership is the capacity to translate vision into reality." A visionary leader needs to establish what matters and articulate why it is important, set direction, and inspire others with their contagious passion and clear purpose.

A friend of mine asked, "If you just turn left at the end of your street and begin driving, what are the chances that you will end up in Phoenix, Arizona?" Actually, the chances hover somewhere around zero. They get much better if you select Phoenix as your destination, get excited enough by the prospect to use Google maps and then plan how to get there. It is the same with leadership. There has to be a destination (vision), an articulated way to get there (purpose) and excitement for the journey (passion).

The Relationship Between Vision and Passion

Vision is one common denominator of successful leaders. It is often the driving force behind their ability to gain influence with followers. If vision is what we see for the future as leaders, passion makes it important. Vision without passion is mechanical, while vision WITH passion can be inspirational.

Most leaders intuitively understand that leadership calls for both passion and vision. According to Steve Moore of Mission Nexus, if passion is limited, a common temptation is to substitute intensity for the real thing. However, teams can spot the difference. With intensity, we communicate, "I really want you to believe this."

On the other hand, passion communicates, "I really believe this." Intensity is marked mostly by emotion; passion is marked mostly by conviction.

While there is a place for intensity in leadership, it can never be a substitute for passion. Leaders with passion transmit it to others and when a team shares the same conviction as the leader, great things can happen.

What Do Passionate Leaders Do?

Have you run across the saying "passion can't be taught, either you have it or it's caught"? Passionate leaders spread passion to others through their love of life, doing new things, taking risks, being motivated, having a sense of urgency, clearly sharing both their values and exuberance and reinventing themselves often. We know them when we see them, and it can be a contagious feeling.

Dr. May Kay, in an article entitled "Great Leaders Ignite Passion" narrows these descriptions of passion down to four main leadership behaviors.

Passionate people are optimistic, have a great story, involve people, and have a simple recharge strategy. I believe these four behaviors do create passion.

Optimistically Tolerant

Leaders that ignite passion habitually practice optimism. Leaders that are passionate are unstoppable. They are positive and they are not crushed by difficulties and daily challenges because they believe they have control over their future. Universally, the leaders I interviewed listed resilience as important.

This optimistic mindset puts a halt to negative thinking and fuels the drive to succeed. To become more passionate, we have to become more tolerant. This is a great way to redirect negative energy. Passionate people deal with their frustration by focusing on what is going right and what is working now in contrast to concentrating on things that are not going as planned. Accepting different opinions or outcomes and leveraging them helps move things forward. Tolerance opens the door for optimism.

Storytelling

A passionate leader tells a compelling story that grabs the attention of people and guides them to see it, feel it, and envision the future. A compelling story is concise, relevant, shows a full understanding of the target audience and speaks directly to it. If the story unfolds in a way that the team can picture their role in the future, they will embrace it. People must become emotionally involved in new ideas and see how they may help implement a change.

Passionate leaders are consummate change agents, imparting their enthusiasm to others so they will believe in the cause. They ignite a trust in others, which in turn causes the team to engage and accomplish their mission. When the story about the destination is understood and clear, followers are able to understand the purpose, know where they fit in, and help drive toward the destination.

Involving People in Passion

The difference between being a passionate doer and a passionate leader is engaging others. People on the team need to become part of the leader's vision instead of going it alone. Passionate leaders know they need to have faith in their team, and they need to do things to impart the passion.

The successful leadership secret here is this: passionate leaders truly endorse people as their most valuable asset and set their own egos aside. Leaders need people to buy in to their passion in order to see and understand the vision enough to accomplish it. Successful leaders surround themselves with equally passionate, knowledgeable experts who will provide solid ideas and suggestions that the leader may not have thought of herself.

A truly passionate leader knows how to connect the heart, as well as the head, of every team member to the overall vision. It is not just about parroting the vision statement; it is about living it.

A Passion Study

We have all observed that people who are successful and achieve great things truly do exude passion. The key is finding what you are truly passionate about. It turns out a personal passion can mean a lot.

Authors Robert Kriegel and Louis Patler cite a study of 1,500 people over 20 years showing the value of finding passions within your life. At the outset of the study, the group was divided into two groups. Group A: 83 percent of the sample, were people embarking on a career chosen for the prospect of making money first in order to do what they want later. Group B: the other 17 percent of the sample, were people who had chosen their career path for the reverse reason; they were going to pursue their passions and what they wanted to do now and would worry about money later. The data showed some startling revelations:

At the end of the 20 years, 101 of the total study population of 1,500 had become millionaires. Of these millionaires, all but one of them, 100 out of 101, were from Group B, the group that had chosen to pursue what they loved, not income.

This study clearly illustrated the benefits and results of finding and focusing on your passions.

I believe that a leader has to have a contagious enthusiasm for what he does and ignite it in others. This is something that I have always practiced, and I am fortunate that it has helped encourage people to want to work with me. I am lucky I had many team members at Luminations who followed me from at least three different companies, and I am fairly certain that one of the reasons is that the love of what I do is contagious. I learned from some masters.

A story from my time at Johnson and Johnson reflects the impact of contagious enthusiasm and passion. Bill McComb was my Group Product Director. He had come from the ad agency world and he was non-traditional in terms of the way he managed. He was a wild, nonconformist who loved the businesses that we worked on. They were a rag tag list of products that did not seem to fit anywhere else in the company.

We didn't have a lot of resources and there was no real unifying thread for us, as we oversaw a myriad of smaller brands that did not link to each other. The portfolio included: Shower to Shower®, Johnson's® pure cotton, KY® Jelly, Clean and Clear® (a newly acquired hair and acne brand), and Purpose® (a small skin care brand that was sold along with prescription Retin-A). All together, we made up only about $70 million dollars out of a billion-dollar company and still Bill fought for us as if we were a huge business.

With his support, we became enthusiastic about acne because acne, and getting rid of it, is so important to teens and their ultimate self-confidence. He inspired us to think big about these businesses, despite our budgets being modest. He encouraged us to find the insight that would help us develop such compelling products and communication that management could not help but give us more funding.

Bill was very successful at J&J. He went on to lead the Tylenol® business, then their medical device group and then he departed to take over Liz Claiborne®. Bill showed me the importance of pulling a team together with passion, inspiring them and always having their backs. It didn't really matter that our brands were small, he always made us feel important.

Since the company saw us as low priority brands, Bill realized that we were all feeling like we didn't matter that much. He used to gel us together by making fun of it, by calling us the "crack of the ass" of J&J because that's all we really were. We got the last dribs and drabs of funding and no support. He actually put a giant plastic butt on his door and labeled it "crack of the ass", and his nameplate was changed to "Head of the Crack of the Ass Group". We knew he was right in the crack with us, because he believed in us and made us believe in ourselves. Not unlike Donna from Sears, he celebrated little victories.

Passion spreads. It drove us to generate those great insights and get the funding nobody thought we could garner, and then grow the heck out of our businesses. The K·Y® brand is probably a $400+ million brand today and the Clean & Clear® brand is reported publicly at close to $1 billion. That's what happens when you are passionate about something; you inspire your team to be passionate, and you are not afraid to let people know how you feel.

In my early days at J&J, I had another inspiring manager named Sue. Sue was in charge of the entire baby marketing division. At the time that I was first working on Johnson's baby, there were not many women in marketing and even fewer women who were actually mothers.

There had been two pregnancies out of 40 or 50 marketers. Well, Sue was a mom herself and immersed in motherhood and nursing and everything that comes with caring for babies. Because of her, everyone on her team became enraptured by motherhood and nursing. At that time, J&J owned a baby feeding brand called Healthflow®.

We were steeped in infants and it felt good to know how much the company cared about moms. I was surrounded by babyhood and I definitely developed baby envy.

In fact, I developed so much baby envy that I began to consider having my second child at that point. Back then, getting pregnant could easily signal a big career risk, but with one little one at home, I knew it was worth it. Plus, what better way to develop a deep understanding of new moms than by becoming a new mom once again?

By the time my maternity leave ended, Sue had moved on and I was chosen as her successor. This was my first time being in charge of the whole Johnson's® baby brand: shampoo, lotion, oil, powder, wipes, diaper rash cream and more. I thought a lot about how Sue had felt about moms and babies and how willing she had been to share her passion.

I looked at the entire department that was still male-dominated and I told management that I would like everyone who recently had a baby to return from maternity leave (they had no paternity leaves then, although happily they do now) to work on my portfolio of Johnson's® baby products. As far as I knew, that was the first time moms on maternity leave were aggressively welcomed back and the first time the Johnson's® baby brand was headed up by new moms and dads.

Fast forward six years to building my own consulting business and I found myself pitching to a company called FEI Women's' Health. They owned the Paragard® Intrauterine Contraceptive Device (IUD), which they had recently acquired. Three men had acquired the IUD license and were going to run the company. They had very high hopes. However, the IUD market in the U.S. was stalling, partly because of unfounded fears.

This was a great product with a not-so-great reputation. I went to pitch the business and suited up in my professional best to unveil my presentation in a wood-paneled and formal conference room in a well-known and well-appointed private equity firm in New York City. It was painfully silent except for the clock ticking on the wall. Then, one of the gentlemen on the panel cleared his throat and said, "Lisa, you haven't done a lot of work in contraception before and we don't think you really understand the market very well so we're not sure we are going to give you the project."

I was momentarily taken back. I really wanted this project so I responded with, "what if I could show you that I understand the market?" They looked at each other and agreed, "well, that could persuade us, we might consider you."

So, I went out to a number of ob/gyn's (obstetricians and gynecologists) to find out why they weren't placing this particular product and identified those doctors who did place it. I interviewed the few women I could locate that actually had an IUD, (remember that incidence of use was low, and it could be considered a private topic) to understand opposing pros and cons.

What I learned in the process was a little scary because there is a complicated multi-step process to select an IUD and then have it inserted. In line with my strong desire to immerse myself in the consumer journey, I thought it was time for me to get an IUD. I asked my doctor to order one. There were two choices at the time: Paragard®, produced by my potential client, and a competitor, Mirena®.

My doctor and I talked it through, and I took notes. I decided, of course, that I was going to choose the Paragard®, then went through the insurance hell of getting it approved. Not surprisingly, the insurer was not very familiar with the subject of IUDs, even though IUDs were likely saving them a lot of money. It took several calls and an escalation to clarify coverage.

I had the IUD placed and learned that there were some bothersome short-term side effects. These issues could have been much less bothersome if I had known what to expect. By the time I went to see the FEI team again, 5 weeks after our initial meeting, I could bring a much deeper understanding of the IUD patient journey in the U.S. market. Due to my commitment to finding out all the information that I could and placing myself in the center of the patient experience, I had a lot to share.

I had a complete presentation on the category and competition prepared including: the barriers to trial, the process of obtaining an IUD and what, as a patient, it was like after having it placed. I knew about the perceptions and misperceptions they were facing and even about potential issues with insurance. I then summarized why they should hire me and my team… and they did! I don't think you could get any more passionate about a product than to truly dig into it and make it your own.

While I am not advocating going this far to understand every consumer, customer or patient journey, I do advocate immersion. It's crucial to become passionate about that product, service, strategy or message, and then share the passion and insights. There will be times when we can't be that customer or consumer but we can always make an effort to walk in their shoes

This passion for the consumer, customer, doctor, or patient inspires lots of ideas about how to make things better, stronger, faster, clearer – not only will you inspire yourself with this kind of passion, hopefully your whole team will catch the passion as well and want to follow.

Leveraging Leadership Concepts – So What Now?

1. Define your vision: for a role, a project, or a team, communicate it early and often.

2. Passion for the vision is necessary: it cannot be replaced with intensity; be sure your passion is real; find a connection so it is.

3. When the team catches your passion, they will follow you: be sure to acknowledge little successes and celebrate along the way; try to do this at least every month or just at the spur of the moment.

THE IMPORTANCE OF EMOTIONAL INTELLIGENCE AND HANDLING VUCA

(Volatility, Uncertainty, Complexity, and Ambiguity)

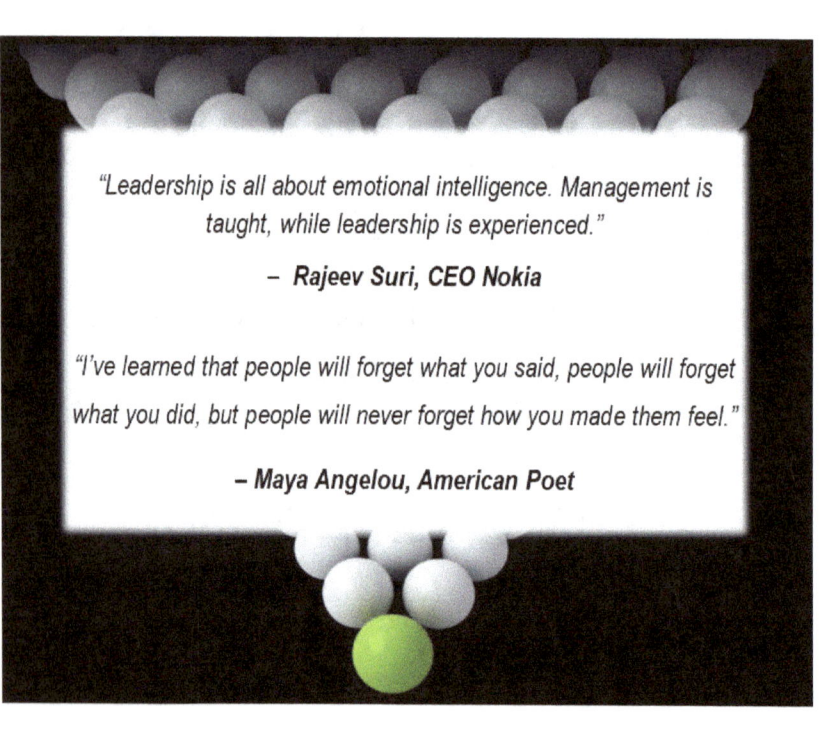

"Leadership is all about emotional intelligence. Management is taught, while leadership is experienced."

– Rajeev Suri, CEO Nokia

"I've learned that people will forget what you said, people will forget what you did, but people will never forget how you made them feel."

– Maya Angelou, American Poet

THE IMPORTANCE OF EMOTIONAL INTELLIGENCE AND HANDLING VUCA

(Volatility, Uncertainty, Complexity, and Ambiguity)

E motional Intelligence is an idea that has taken root in popular culture over the past few decades. At a basic level, its definition is "the capacity to be aware of, control, and express one's emotions, and to handle interpersonal relationships empathetically".

It is thought to be the key to both personal and professional success. This is one of the key shifts I have observed in leadership requirements. We used to look for leaders who commanded, but today, leadership happens only with Emotional Intelligence.

Many years ago, I read an article in *Time* about a Stanford University study created to test the importance of Intelligence Quotient (IQ) or Emotional Intelligence (EI). The study was simple. They recruited 4- and 5-year old children, took them into a room and showed them a plate with one marshmallow on it. The researcher then explained that the children could eat the marshmallow now, or they could wait to eat it while the researcher ran an errand. The children knew that the researchers preferred that they wait and control their impulses. When the researcher returned, if the child had waited, he/she could then have two marshmallows instead of just the one presently on the plate.

The study tracked which children were able to wait and earn the two marshmallows and which ones couldn't wait and gobbled up the single marshmallow before the researcher returned to the room. What they found was surprising. **The children who were willing to delay gratification and waited to receive the second marshmallow, ended up having higher school scores,** lower levels of substance abuse, lower likelihood of obesity, and better responses to stress over time.

The researchers felt that those who could delay gratification had the building blocks of Emotional Intelligence. They also understood the potential importance and rewards of waiting and controlling impulses, especially unproductive ones.

What makes this research exceptional is that the researchers followed each child for more than 40 years, and the group who waited patiently for the second marshmallow, succeeded in whatever capacity they were measuring. In other words, this series of experiments proved that the ability to delay gratification was critical for success in life and essentially proved that Emotional Intelligence was a far better indicator of future success than IQ.

Jason Barnett, Vice Chairman of RXR Realty and my baby brother, feels that Emotional Intelligence is imperative in leadership and in success in general. "One of my strengths is that I can often read the other side in a negotiation. Understanding is important to relationship building. Emotional Intelligence gives you the ability to adjust to the other party and that stops stalemates. It also enables leaders to know when people need support."

Applying Emotional Intelligence Through VUCA

VUCA is a concept that originated with students at the U.S. Army War College to describe the volatility, uncertainty, complexity, and ambiguity of the world after the Cold War. The concept gained new relevance to characterize our current business and world environment. It included the unique leadership skills, with a well-developed sense of Emotional Intelligence, required to navigate it successfully.

Comfort with addressing VUCA is an increasingly important leadership skill. This is another one of the shifts in leadership essentials that I have witnessed over time. Navigating vast uncertainty with confidence has become critical for strong leaders. Where once this skill may have been rarely deployed, today it's a regular need.

Physical VUCA

During my time as CEO of Netgrocer, I was managing in an almost constant state of uncertainty and ambiguity. It was a fundamental learning period. We faced uncertainty both from the financial volatility of the company and several external and internal crises that included the attacks on 9/11 and a massive theft of information. VUCA was my daily challenge.

I will never forget that Tuesday in September, in 2011. It was a beautiful sunny day. We had scheduled a leadership team meeting in our warehouse in North Brunswick, New Jersey later that morning. The plan was that our Manhattan team would join us at around 10am.

As Netgrocer was founded by an Israeli entrepreneur, many on my management team were Israeli. My CIO, Ari Sabah, had checked on everything at the Manhattan office. Then he left, and he was driving toward the Holland Tunnel to come out to New Jersey when he was shocked to see something unusual.

I got that fateful phone call. It was Ari saying "Lisa, I'm going to be late. It's basically a case of completely stopped traffic, and we don't know why. The sky is covered with fluttering pink paper. We can't even see; there's no visibility. I think one of the World Trade Towers was hit by a plane."

Much later, we would learn that that the pink fluttering storm was thousands and thousands of those pink phone message sheets from every office in the Twin Towers being blown out of the buildings in the inferno.

At that point, we didn't know the extent of the tragedy. We just shrugged and realized that Ari was going to be late to the team meeting. Ari said he thought it was only a small plane that had brushed the World Trade Center and he was going to continue on to New Jersey to join the meeting.

Then the next plane hit and the rest of my leadership team who were with me in North Brunswick concluded, "This is not an accident. This is terrorism." Now, at the time, everybody else still thought it was an accident. News commentators hypothesized either a problem with air traffic control or equipment. Nobody else thought that it could possibly be intentional, yet.

My team remained firm. "We think it's intentional". Being from Israel, I knew they had been trained to expect the unexpected and to be a bit more cynical and skeptical than I was, so I knew it was important to listen to them. I had never really experienced anything like this, but I trusted them, and preparing for the worst meant we called Ari back and directed him to return to our NYC office and take care of the people there. Ari turned around and went back through the smoke to the Manhattan office at 11 Broadway, in full view of the former towers.

As the events unfolded, it became obvious that it was, in fact, a terror attack. Our office on Broadway was only a few blocks from the explosions. The first thing we had to do was figure out how to ensure people's safety and whether we were going to evacuate them. If so, to where should we evacuate? Later, we had to decide about the sustainability of the business itself, as all of our servers were housed at 11 Broadway, very close to the epicenter of this tragedy. This was early in the infancy of Ecommerce and there had really been very little discussion about technology redundancy. We had made the mistake of keeping all of the servers in one vulnerable location.

However, as we watched in disbelief as both Towers came disintegrating down, our thoughts were not about the technology, but about the people. We knew we needed to evacuate everyone, but there was no way to get them out of downtown New York by car or train. All roads around the building were filled with people and debris and many were blocked. What to do wasn't a question but how we could do it was.

After Ari returned to the office, he locked up the building and led the evacuation. Everyone walked across the Brooklyn Bridge. It was an anxious time for them, and I didn't hear about that journey until about a day and a half later because we also lost cell coverage. Then we lost Internet coverage, and the entire power grid shut down in downtown New York.

I had never faced such a terrifying event before, and this was a defining moment for me as a leader. Thankfully, I was able to trust my team, who had been trained for an event like this. It was very fortuitous that I had a team of former Israeli military to bounce ideas off of, and I was able to act quickly and decisively. Our country had rarely experienced this level of terrorism before. Without this team and their training, I might have been much less decisive and made even more mistakes than I did.

With the power shut down, our business was shut down. We had to reconnect and figure out our plan and strategy for business continuation. Although we did have a team in New Jersey, we didn't have the T-1 line that we needed for the high-speed internet access that would allow us to run the business from there. There was no way to communicate with our customers. To complicate things, we were without power in the Manhattan office for eight days. However, Con-Ed (NYC's power company) placed power trailers in the streets and we were able to snake wires up to the eighth floor so we could restart our servers and turn the Netgrocer website back on. Within a few days, we were back in business.

The danger and uncertainty were like nothing else I had ever faced. People came first - they matter more than anything else. In a frightening or uncertain situation, it's important to let them know this. Communicate. In times of crisis, people are hungry for information. I also needed to trust some of the other experts on my team, who had dealt with terrorism situations in their past lives. It was a powerful lesson in learning how to develop the most effective plan to get us back into business quickly without jeopardizing anyone's lives or livelihood.

What I did then and what I did in many other volatile situations, is communicated with everybody, regularly. I shared, "here's what we know, here's what we don't know, here's our plan." I always asked if anybody had alternative suggestions. I would then come to a decision and make sure everyone had clear roles and next steps. This helped us stabilize quickly. Of course, on September 11th, the most important next step was to let everybody know that the New York team was safe.

Later I would have to decide if they should go back into that office in downtown NYC, while there were still smoldering fires at the World Trade Center site. We were forced to acknowledge that the only way to continue to operate was to send them back to the office. I also knew, that as a leader, if I was going to make my team go into that office and walk past the destruction of the World Trade Center to do it, I should be with them.

So, I moved my office to New York City for a couple of months after 9/11. To do that, I had to figure out how to get downtown every day, when subways weren't running anymore, and the few trains available were unpredictable. The trek was a many-block walk from the closest train station. When I did arrive, it was worth it. I felt as if I needed to be there, because I believe a good leader shows up for her team.

To be allowed to work downtown, the U.S. Army required special identification cards. Everyone working downtown faced a number of hardships. One awful memory I have is walking by hundreds of signs seeking missing loved ones. The buildings and streets were covered in a thick veil of dust. The air was thick with a noxious smell. Smoldering hulks of metal were visible from our building, and first responders were working by the hundreds, on the massive pile of rubble. Despite the horrors, hope hadn't been given up yet and everyone thought people might still be found alive. We later learned this was not the case.

On our street, just a block or so away from the pile, business began to re-ignite. Office doors were permanently open as those giant cables, coming from temporary power trailers with generators, snaked into each stairwell. Military troops with guns and even tanks patrolled the area. It was not a friendly or easy work environment. I hope that my willingness to be on the ground with them, close to the Twin Towers, helped us get through a volatile time. In retrospect, none of us should probably have been there, together or not. We didn't understand the health risks, so we made the best call we could at the time.

Financial VUCA

Like physical uncertainty, financial uncertainty can mean job volatility. That's an equally scary thing for people. Everybody knew, at Netgrocer, that we had not yet raised enough capital to get to profitability. Going public had ceased to be an option after the economic bubble burst.

As we came to the end of our cash, people in various functions knew they were doing things to stretch it, like paying suppliers a day or two later than before or deferring purchases. I was calling three or four suppliers a day to negotiate better terms and everyone was carefully counting pennies.

If we could hold off and make do with lower levels of inventory, then we could stretch our funds. My team knew that things were challenging, and they wanted to know how serious it was.

As with other uncertainty, my approach was to call everyone together and tell them exactly how challenging things were and what we were doing about it. The company was down to about a million dollars in its coffers. We had 110 people working in the warehouse, plus another 40 or so professionals who needed to be paid weekly for their work.

I told them exactly where we were financially and what our plan was to deplete the cash more slowly than originally planned. I outlined a roadmap to raise that next round of capital or seek outside investment and was honest about the risks.

We did have some outside investors interested and we also were launching programs with some major retailers that would generate the kind of publicity that would enable us to get to profitability quickly.

I actually showed them the timeline and told them specifically what we were going to do about the financial issues. I continued to keep them informed, at each transition point every month, where we were on that original timeline.

By working as a team and by my communicating honestly, we were able to stave off a financial crisis. We did ultimately sell the company. We split it in half - the software division went to a company called MyWebGrocer and the online grocery business went to Wakefern, which owns ShopRite® in the Northeast part of the U.S.

However, getting to this end conclusion did take longer than we thought. During that time, we had to make some very tough decisions, one of which was that we couldn't supply certain products to certain people. We couldn't afford the inventory with suppliers who demanded payment faster than we could supply the cash. Another was that we had to forego the opportunity to launch a major partnership with Amazon. We would have become the online grocery provider nationally for Amazon, but we knew that, in order to turn that program on, we would immediately need an extra $2 million in inventory to serve those customers. Without funding, we had no choice but to defer the Amazon program. This was another tough call but the right thing to do, financially, at the time.

This experience taught me a lot about how to lead in an environment of financial uncertainty. I learned that frequent, open communication, without fear, was the best way to show the team how much I cared. By being pragmatic and clear, it helped create a situation where nobody left the company, even knowing that they were at great risk of losing their jobs. Nobody stopped doing his or her job either. If anything, they worked harder to try to get us to where we needed to be.

Clear, understandable communication matters a lot. I believe that my sincere confidence and optimism helped. I saw a light at the end of the dark tunnel and made sure they saw it too. Today, most business teams operate in an ambiguous environment with much uncertainty. Navigating VUCA well can mean the difference between success and failure.

My Luminations team typically demonstrated effective communication. The VUCA we experienced as consultants is different and equally demanding, but often driven by uncertain or conflicting requests that we wanted to honor. We required a clear and concise brief for any work we did. This helped us align on the objective. We checked in often with each other and our clients as well. Everyone's time is precious, so we strove to give all the information that is needed to make a decision, but not to overwhelm. Keeping our clients in mind meant we communicated frequently, reassuring with information and updates, and taking the pressure off them. We thought about what's would overdeliver for them without overcomplicating in any way.

On a major competitive analysis project, we researched nine different competitors in the smart home industry, and we didn't have a lot of time to do it. The project was complex because there were lots of different data sources and many new Luminations people involved. To ensure everyone on the team knew what they were supposed to, we put in writing exactly what we needed people to look at and showed them how to populate a standard template (e.g. what they needed to research and learn about each competitor).

We took the time to share our ultimate objective, how it would benefit our client, and answer questions up front. We provided some examples of where to find the information and laid out key resources. Then we sent them off to work. All information needed to be right and it needed to be clearly sourced. We were honest about the timeline pressure. Today Artificial Intelligence might help alleviate a lot of this pressure. By giving people a clear picture of what we expected, our roadmap, and an outline of the deliverable, we got what was expected and more. We set a clear vision and expectations, and the journey was much smoother. If the team did not have that clear picture, we could easily end up with poor results and wasted time.

Telling the truth is the best way to lead. Being clear on what's happening and needs to happen mitigates those risks or concerns. Be honest because your team or your employees are going to figure it out anyway. "I don't think there's anything more important than helping people understand risk so they can band together to drive success", shared my VUCA expert, Tom Weck. **Good leaders step up and admit uncertainty, ambiguity and daunting challenges and leverage the strengths of their teams.**

Leaders also need to express confidence that they will figure out a way to get the team to success. Even if you are not feeling completely confident yourself, as a leader you want to inspire your team to continue to do the work they need to do. Success breeds success. If people are afraid, they are often not committed. A strong leader doesn't ignore what's happening, he or she is sure to let the team know, "I got this - we'll figure it out". It is also important to acknowledge and remind people that they are valued and part of the solution.

How Emotional Intelligence Translates into Coping with VUCA

Remember the marshmallow study? Emotional Intelligence included self-awareness, self-management and empathy, which translates into good communication skills. When you put all of these emotionally intelligent qualities together, it forms a great path forward to develop a good leader.

Decades of research now point to Emotional Intelligence as being the critical factor that sets star performers apart from the rest of the pack. The connection is so strong that 90 percent of top performers have been shown to have high Emotional Intelligence. Emotional Intelligence, real empathy, affects how we manage behavior, navigate social complexities, and make personal decisions to achieve positive results.

Having high Emotional Intelligence means that you have the capacity to empathize with your team and understand their motivations. This ability is especially important in times of high stress and in emergency situations like the aftermath of 9/11 or Covid shutdown. Being able to operate in all aspects of VUCA (Volatility, Uncertainty, Complexity, and Ambiguity) while maintaining Emotional Intelligence is a true leadership skill that will set you apart.

VUCA in the Entrepreneurial World and COVID

We didn't realize how important this would be until early 2020. I was in year seventeen of leading my boutique innovation and consulting firm, Luminations. Our work was about solving complex challenges for clients and it relied heavily on face-to-face strategy sessions and high-trust team dynamics. When COVID-19 hit, how we delivered this changed overnight.

Projects were postponed. Clients froze budgets. My team—scattered across time zones—was suddenly anxious, and disoriented. Although we'd been working remotely for years, morale dipped, and I could feel the undercurrent of fear: Were we going to survive this?

I felt the weight of every payroll cycle. But I also knew this was a leadership moment that would define who we were. I gathered the team on Zoom (we were seasoned virtual workers but at the time we had been relying on Webex and Skype), not to present a plan, but to listen. I asked, "What do you need most right now—from me, from each other?" The answers weren't about strategy. The answers were about human needs, first and foremost health and safety and then clarity, connection, and stability.

So, we adapted. We scrapped our roadmap and co-created a new operating model—shorter sprints, daily standups, clear boundaries between work and rest. Weekly town halls became a ritual, a space where we shared wins and worries alike. I brought in virtual guest speakers such as clients, clinicians, and friends, as a way to keep morale and curiosity alive.

At the same time, we had to rethink what mattered most—not just for us, but for our clients. In this environment, we couldn't cling to old priorities. For one client in luxury home lighting, half their business was commercial and was completely stalled. The other half, residential, was booming as people invested in their home environments. We partnered to help them pivot strategies and resources toward DTC channels and reallocate focus accordingly. Our health care clients needed to build supply and reach consumers and patients with more reassurance than ever before. Our food clients found new opportunities as everyone began eating at home. Our tech clients found time to educate and innovate where they'd previously been lagging for customers. Just think about all the technologies that were adopted to enhance productivity and help us to live our lives safely during COVID.

Despite uncertainty and broken supply chains, most clients had to find ways to scale quickly. It wasn't about optimizing processes anymore—it was about getting critical products out the door, fast. We helped triage their operations and mobilize around that singular goal.

These weren't just consulting projects anymore—they were lifelines. And we had to meet the moment with the same courage we asked of our clients. The turning point for me came when a senior consultant, visibly burned out, told me she felt like she was failing, really struggling. I paused, then shared my own challenges, such as my sleepless nights, self-doubt, and concerns about not doing enough or maybe trying to do too much. That vulnerability shifted something for her and for me. It gave others permission to be real, too. Most of our weekly meetings involved a lot of crying. From that moment on, our culture, always empathetic, became more caring, more honest, and much more resilient.

By late 2020, not only had we retained our entire team, we managed to grow our business by +30%. More importantly, we came through it stronger because we had worked together.

The early days of Covid taught me that leadership isn't about having the right answers. It's about helping others focus on the right questions. It's about creating the conditions for people to do their best work—even in the worst of times. And sometimes, the most powerful thing a leader can say is: "I don't know either, but I'm here with you and we can figure it out together."

Leveraging Leadership Concepts - So What Now?

1. Emotional Intelligence (EI) is essential to leadership growth: check your empathy level and personal connections to do even better. If you aren't really listening and identifying with your team or consumer, immerse yourself. Ask how you can understand even more.

2. Get comfortable with VUCA: proactively take on a project that's ambiguous or join a team with an uncertain future. Deliberately move out of your comfort zone and move forward successfully anyway. Find at least one project like this if it's not already in your responsibilities.

3. Anyone can navigate a calm sea: the successful leaders need to be able to operate in uncertainty. Leverage what you learn in #2 ultimately to lead an uncertain group or team facing VUCA.

SET THE GOAL, SURROUND YOURSELF WITH EXPERTS – THEN DELEGATE

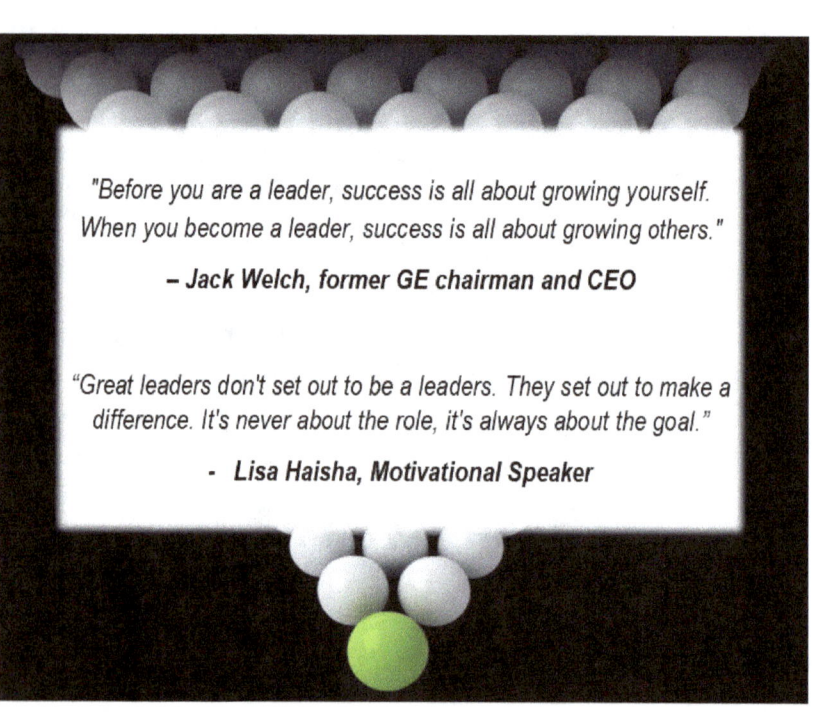

"Before you are a leader, success is all about growing yourself. When you become a leader, success is all about growing others."

– Jack Welch, former GE chairman and CEO

"Great leaders don't set out to be a leaders. They set out to make a difference. It's never about the role, it's always about the goal."

- Lisa Haisha, Motivational Speaker

SET THE GOAL, SURROUND YOURSELF WITH EXPERTS – THEN DELEGATE

Being an effective leader does not mean being an expert in everything. In fact, a good leader knows how to define what is needed, attract the right talent, and motivate them to work together to attain the goal of the team. A leader needs to be comfortable in her own skin and not be threatened by the experts on the team.

We have to rely on experts, those who know more about a topic than we do. Tom Weck was the expert I relied on while completing the herculean Johnson's baby task at Johnson & Johnson. When I interviewed him for this book, his words of wisdom were, "As I get older, I'm almost less certain of things and much more likely to solicit feedback and input from others. I know I made mistakes in judgment earlier in my career because I didn't always gather a diversity of opinions."

I was reminded of the value of calling in the experts a few years back, as my team and I were working for a wonderful brand of natural skin care products called Korres. Most of their ingredients came from new applications of undiscovered plant extracts. In this instance, it was important to bring in botanists and scientists who understood plant extracts and what they could do for human skin. The expert wasn't a dermatologist or a cosmetologist, but somebody who was thinking about rare plants and trying to discover what hadn't been discovered yet.

Without these experts, new ingredients and their benefits would not have been revealed. We couldn't uncover new ingredients alone; instead we had to attract and lean on our experts, and shamelessly pursue new knowledge to innovate and grow the business. I found I needed to learn enough to know what questions to ask. It was not up to me to know everything, just to ask the right questions. I've already discussed how valuable my software and technical experts were to me at Netgrocer. One, our Chief Technology Officer, Yair Avgar, now teaches cybersecurity and big data at Columbia and he's still my go-to resource for new technology.

We're Not Alone

When it comes to leadership, realize that no one person can do everything. It's impossible to succeed alone. As a lone entrepreneur or a small start-up team, there is sometimes a temptation to try to do everything by yourself. There is always a way, even with limited funds, to leverage the help of a team.

In order to know what is needed, we go back to those clearly-defined goals. What is the purpose of the team or project, what do they need to accomplish, and what indicators will mean we have achieved those goals? When these aspects are clearly defined, it is easy to then determine what type of team members will make the team successful. Decide how best to recruit this crew and bring them on board, making sure each person understands that they bring a unique expertise to the table.

Case Study

Netgrocer was founded in 1987 by an Israeli entrepreneur, Uri Evan. He planned to create the first online nationwide supermarket. (Keep in mind this was WAY before Amazon, in the earliest stages of online shopping).

I began as head of marketing at Netgrocer, when the concept of ordering online was definitely in its infancy. There were some changes in management, and I was called to move into the role of CEO just in time for outside forces to cause the near implosion of the company.

The owner was smart enough to know his vision was not gaining ground quickly enough. The company needed revenue and recognition fast. Through brainstorming, we were able to create the concept of the Endless

Aisle®. The insight was uncovered because we found shoppers and retailers alike were coming to Netgrocer to find their hard-to-find favorite items. These were products that consumers were demanding but were hard to keep stocked at a local retail store because the demand was uneven. For example, Jell-O® brand gelatin has over 50 different flavors. However, most stores would only stock 10 or fewer of the more popular flavors. If someone wanted their favorite Island Pineapple flavor, the store would have to special order a whole case for their customer. If no one else happened to want this flavor, the balance of the case might go to waste.

By uncovering this fact, we also uncovered a huge opportunity. While Netgrocer had been initially conceived as a way for consumers to order regular weekly groceries online and get home delivery, we could now see the possibilities of using the same model to give consumers the ability to order their hard-to-find items from anywhere in the world. These items, chosen by consumers, could arrive ostensibly, from their local store—and the Endless Aisle® was born.

The Endless Aisle® in a nutshell, was software that allowed a local brick and mortar retailer to show its own customers 30,000 more products than they carried in the physical store. Shoppers could order these items from their own local grocery store instead of going to a competitor. Retailers and manufacturers could fulfill loyal customers' wishes without managing complex special orders.

Soon, manufacturers were offering their full lines of products to us and directing consumers our way. Netgrocer became the only place in the country that stocked every Jell-O® or Crystal Lite® flavor and every form and SKU of Similac® baby formula. If you wanted Quisp® cereal, the only way to get it was to come to us. Word was starting to spread.

We decided to pitch this idea to Stop and Shop® (an Ahold grocery chain) and after many heartfelt discussions and trips to Quincy, Massachusetts, they said "Well, we will give it a try, but only if you put physical ordering kiosks in our store." Stop & Shop® management wanted people coming into the store, not just shopping online. They needed the traffic and we desperately needed a major retailer to sign on for our Endless Aisle® software solution. We needed it because, without it, we would not have been able to gain further investment in the company and sustain the business for the future.

This was no small challenge, since this was back in 2001 and the U.S. didn't have well-developed broadband service around the country yet. Touch pads and kiosks were relatively new to the world. At that time, if a customer could not find what he or she was looking for in their favorite store, they would leave and go to the competition or minimally be frustrated by their local store. Stop & Shop® wanted to avoid losing this customer. They needed to keep her in the store, have her place the immediate order and have it shipped directly to her home.

As mentioned, Ahold's stipulation for the publicized licensing of our software was that we would have to place digital ordering kiosks in Stop & Shop® stores. We would have to integrate our system and theirs. These kiosks printed a receipt for customers to take to the cash register for their special order. We had to develop and perfect new platforms in just three months. We had no choice, so we had to make it happen.

I brought it to the Netgrocer team with confidence, even though I had never done anything like this before and our Information Technology (IT) people hadn't either. However, as a leader, I knew I had a team of experts and problem solvers to support me.

While we had custom-developed the ordering software, we had no idea if we could make an interface that was simple enough to use on a touch screen or a kiosk keyboard. Plus, most of these stores didn't have wireless or even wired Internet service yet so we'd have to install that for them, too. As a team, we had to figure out how, not if, we'd make it happen. We also offered clear and confident communication, a detailed roadmap, and a heavy dose of optimism.

We sourced the kiosks, coded the software, installed cabling and Internet in some of the stores and, after troubleshooting, it worked beautifully. It came to fruition partly because we just believed we could do it. That team worked day and night to develop it. Then we all went into the stores and worked 24/7 staffing those new kiosks to make sure that if anything went wrong, it was fixed fast. Early prototyping and ongoing optimization helped. This approach is a cornerstone of rapid innovation, now often called agile.

Fortunately, not too much went wrong. This was because our technology team was stellar, they knew what they were doing, and they worked non-stop to accomplish our vision. When Stop & Shop® publicly announced its partnership expansion with Netgrocer's Endless Aisle®, lots of other chains in the grocery retail world clamored for it. That's exactly what we needed in order to thrive.

Finding the Team

At Netgrocer, I was lucky enough to have an expert team in place from the beginning. However, we have often have to begin by forming an initial team.

In the concept of building a good business team, experts usually agree on two things: 1) the leader needs to define what skills they lack and look for team members who are experts in these areas and 2) he or she must clearly define roles.

Jason Barnett, Vice Chairman of RXR Realty, is a firm believer in building teams of experts. "If I look around the room and I'm the smartest one there, then I know I have the wrong people in the room. While you need to have the self-confidence to apply what you do know, don't be afraid to ask questions." In leadership, asking probing questions is often more important than answering them.

Once specific expertise is outlined, it is important to take that one step further and clearly define the role of each team member. Confusion caused by undefined roles can weaken morale and ultimately cause the team to fail in reaching their goals.

I always look for people who have skills that I don't have so I can really stretch my imagination and my brain. They have to be willing to challenge me without restraint. This can take them a bit of time to realize, as traditional models of leadership tend to be more authoritarian.

To the inexperienced leader, the expectation is that team members will comply without question. I have found that the best team members always have questions to ask.

The more experience I get, the more I realize the value of people who are more knowledgeable than I am on topics that will complement my strategy. Their questions make me think differently and engender better decisions. Jason would say that people who know more than we do are imperative to success and most of my podcast guests recommend creating a personal board of directors.

Last, but certainly not least, is the importance of finding team members who share my passion for the project. Someone can be an expert in a particular field, but if she does not buy into the concept of the business or project, she will not apply herself to ensure success. My own enthusiasm is always more powerful when it can feed off others who have it too.

Listening to the Team

While challenging your leadership is important, it is often frowned upon. This is usually a shame. I have seen many companies recently allowing the whim of someone in senior leadership to swing the whole organization. Nobody wants to take the risk of speaking up in an environment where job security may feel unattainable. I see this a lot when a senior executive just doesn't realize the impact his or her question or comment has on the team.

Employees may be too afraid to point out that the direction is not based on data or the customer or that it doesn't feel right. In Start-Up Nation: The Story of Israel's Economic Miracle by Dan Senor and Saul Singer, we are reminded that cultures that encourage this type of healthy challenge to authority often innovate fastest.

In some companies, people don't challenge authority. This happened to me at a large company with a crazy decision made around what color a bottle should be for a new consumer product.

The leader of the team did not like the color orange for a particular product, even though the orange packaging had tested well with consumers via statistically significant shelf testing. The product prototypes had already been shown to retailers and the winning designs were orange. This senior leader just didn't want something orange so asked that it be changed to another color. His choice was a very pale color that only caused the product to get lost on the shelf and hence lost in the marketplace. He had made it clear that he wasn't interested in other points of view.

They lost a lot of money, mostly because the people below him didn't have the courage to say "we have data that says orange is going to work," or "you are entitled to your opinion but it is contradictory to what we learned." That same senior executive wasn't around after the launch failed. The retailers were angry because it wasn't what they had been shown and consumers didn't buy it. It cost $50 million to launch and it became a wasted investment because no one wanted to take the risk of contradicting the color preference of a senior leader.

To put it bluntly, there is no point in forming a team if, as leader, you are not willing to listen to what they have to say. It is important to create a climate that encourages everyone to speak up. If there is a disagreement on what path to follow going forward, and there's bound to be, do it respectfully and with full disclosure.

One of my most-admired leaders in the consumer goods space is Carla Vernón, who was the Natural & Organic Operating Unit President at General Mills and today is CEO of the Honest Company. She believes that it is important to create a culture that attracts great talent, accepts a diversity of voices and, most importantly, fosters senior leaders who are comfortable with "collaboration not continuous agreement."

The top three qualities Carla looks for in a potential leader are: "courage, collaboration and curiosity." "We are in a time when few things are assured, so leaders now have to make decisions despite uncertainty. (We have to make) decisions that are grounded on courage, bold actions and the acceptance of potential risk."

"When it comes to building teams, the marketplace is so complex it is imperative that leaders create an environment that fosters collaboration. I have worked with leaders who have the descriptor "plays well with others" as their top criterion for selecting new hires. In both leaders and team members, curiosity is a must to maintain your lead in a complex and changing marketplace – always ask the question "what can we learn?"

Delegating to the Team

One of the biggest lessons I learned as an emerging leader was the importance of delegation. It was as a new CEO of Netgrocer that I truly understood the value of managing a team of people who were smarter than I was.

I was working for the first time in a technology organization and almost every function did something that I did not fully understand. The bad news was I had to work with a lot of people in a lot of areas where I had limited knowledge; and the good news was I had to work in a lot of areas where I had limited knowledge.

Looking at it from both angles, the unknown can be scary. The positive side and what I almost always view as a benefit, was that I was forced to learn, and forced to trust.

I had never built software before, I had never managed a warehouse before, and I had never had clients at the level of CEO before - all new challenges. In all cases, I had to learn to trust and delegate to the functional leads on my team and I had to learn as much as I could, as quickly as I could to contribute to their actions.

Learning the Art of Delegation

Delegation is the ultimate form of scaling an organization. When we are limited by time, resources or the lack of knowledge, an intelligent team leader has no choice but to delegate. This enables more to be done by the best people.

Unfortunately, many new managers think that delegation is simply the art of giving orders in a civilized way. Delegation is really the art of learning how to communicate and motivate. If someone gets promoted because she did things well, that does not automatically translate into knowing how to delegate. In more junior roles, we might get away with doing the work ourselves. Moving up in responsibility means we have to make room for others to step in. As a leader, our job is to understand the goal of the team, communicate that goal effectively, inspire the team to achieve that goal and remove any obstacles keeping them from attaining success.

In her book, Learning How to Delegate as a Leader, Esther Schindler tells the story of entrepreneur Doug Kisgen, who was hired right out of school to develop recycling programs for a phone book company and handle the promotion of this program.

"My boss had put together a program right before I started," says Kisgen. "Unfortunately, no one showed up for the press conference. It was a flop." New-guy Kisgen handled the next market release, including a successful press conference. "Imagine my surprise when my supervisor called me shortly after the media blitz to inform me that I would never be allowed to schedule press conferences again. Evidently, he looked at my success, compared to his previous failure, and thought I made him look bad. I couldn't believe it."

"A huge part of delegation is realizing that when those to whom we delegate succeed, we succeed, too," concludes Kisgen. "In fact, our biggest hope when delegating should be that others do things better than us. This is precisely why we delegate in the first place."

Summing It All Up

Mari Baker, former President of BabyCenter and current corporate board member, said that, to her, one of the most important aspects of leadership is reinforcing the importance of EQ (empathy) - being able to relate, understand, communicate and connect with a team without being authoritarian.

"There can be so much chaos with a team that you need to provide clarity, but not in a command and control construct. It is important to communicate in a way that rallies and inspires but does not dictate."

A good leader will know how to recruit the right people for the team to ensure they can reach the goal, won't be intimidated by experts, will learn delegation as an art form and will understand that individual successes ensure the success of the entire team. Seeing others' successes, not as a threat, but as a marker of your own success, means you've set yourself up as a leader that people will definitely want to follow.

Leveraging Leadership Concepts - So What Now?

1. Don't shy away from experts – seek those who complement your strengths and lean on their expertise. Recruit your own personal Board of Directors to help you succeed, find at least 2 of these folks in the next 2-3 months.

2. Don't squelch your team's challenges – take them seriously, ask questions, pivot when necessary.

3. Delegation means we need others to succeed for and with us; break down barriers so those who work for or with you can succeed, remind your team that you will do this for them.

COMMUNICATE, COMMUNICATE, COMMUNICATE, AND CONFIRM

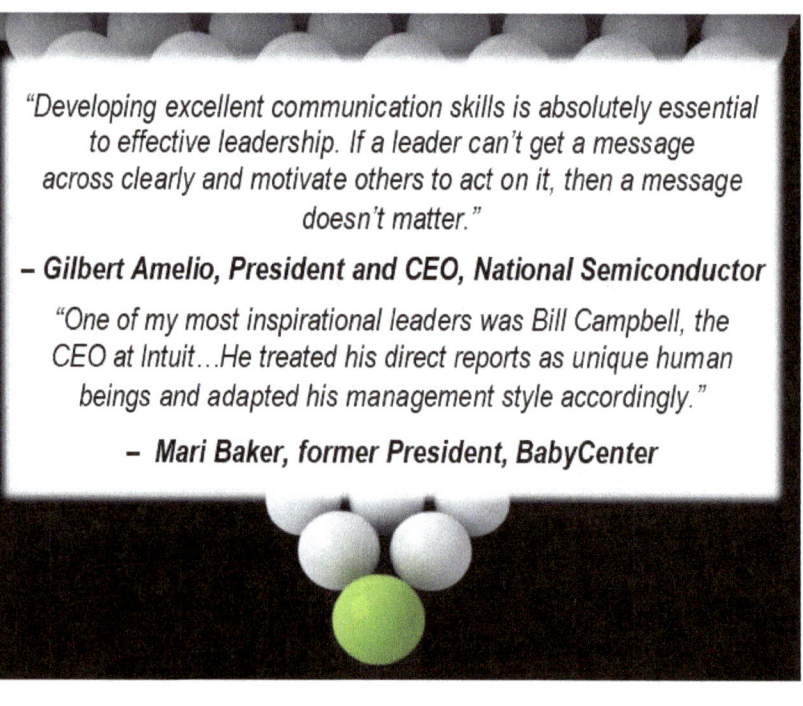

"Developing excellent communication skills is absolutely essential to effective leadership. If a leader can't get a message across clearly and motivate others to act on it, then a message doesn't matter."

– Gilbert Amelio, President and CEO, National Semiconductor

"One of my most inspirational leaders was Bill Campbell, the CEO at Intuit...He treated his direct reports as unique human beings and adapted his management style accordingly."

– Mari Baker, former President, BabyCenter

COMMUNICATE, COMMUNICATE, COMMUNICATE, AND CONFIRM

Remember the childhood game of telephone? A group of friends would line up, the first person would whisper something to the second person, who would in turn whisper it to the next person and so on until the final person got a version of the message? The last person would then say out loud what he thought he'd heard and then the first person would repeat the original message – and lots of laughter would ensue when the two messages would be miles apart in meaning.

Unfortunately, this game happens all too often in business. Most people want to be clear but all too often the message is garbled, and the end result is rarely a laugh.

A modern-day version of this story is the complexity of using texts and email. If not careful, they can both be a very one-dimensional form of communication and can be fraught with mismatched expectations and assumptions. It's so difficult to communicate any nuance or intended tone. Sometimes it just pays to pick up the phone or arrange a face-to-face conversation.

For leaders, a top priority should be making sure that clear communication happens at all levels of an organization and a project. In my son's textbook for his Emergency Medical Services (EMS) training, I saw a graphic that illustrated the definition of communication. Focusing on radio usage, it showed a sender, a receiver and a message. EMS protocol is that the sender confirms that the receiver has gotten the communication and checks for comprehension by asking that it be repeated back.

The receiver always confirms receipt with an "affirm" or a "received" as well. No communication, no matter how simple, goes unacknowledged and this ensures that comprehension is clear, even in the midst of a crisis situation. In business, keep in mind that confirming understanding and checking for comprehension is the most important part of the process.

A friend of mine tells the story of something as simple as a restaurant reservation. She had called and asked for a 5:30pm reservation for four people. Then plans changed slightly, so she called back to see if she could change the reservation to 5. She and her party arrived at the restaurant at 5pm, and asked to be seated at a booth.

The hostess told them that they could not sit in a booth, as it would not accommodate 5 people. After a few puzzled glances, the light dawned. The hostess thought the reservation went from 4 people to 5, when the intent was to move from 5:30pm to 5pm.

Establishing clear communication, checking for comprehension and doing timely follow-ups are all important aspects of communication in business. In simple terms, good communication is the ability to articulate, either verbally or visually, what we need, want and expect. On the flip side, it also includes listening well and checking for comprehension. We need to be able to hear what it being said, even what is not being said, and interpret it correctly.

Next, we must rapidly take that interpretation and translate it into a response, a solution or a plan. In my early years at Johnson & Johnson, everyone was required to take a course on active listening. We learned how to restate what we'd heard and check for understanding. This was the critical component of the class and most interactions subsequently involved a restatement, making communication clearer and easier, especially if the topic was emotional or difficult.

Truly successful communication is also inspirational, and it makes people want to do what they need to do as opposed to dreading it. Communication shouldn't manipulate but it can motivate.

Case Study

During my time at Nestle, my manager assigned me to create the holiday/Christmas cookbook for the year. At the time, recipe cookbooks, sold along with Toll House Morsels®, were key drivers of chocolate and baking ingredient sales. His direction, "work with the test kitchens to create 100 new recipes." I was pretty junior but thought I was up for the task. I briefed the chefs and then began a months-long journey of 9am recipe tastings and evaluations. We were close to the deadline for laying out the cookbook for publication and I proudly presented it to my boss, ready for a big pat on the back for all the team effort and creativity.

Instead I faced an onslaught of criticism. Why? Apparently one of the key goals for this cookbook was to feature and promote our newest items. This hadn't been clearly communicated and I hadn't asked enough questions to ensure clarity. Among our 100 recipes, only 7 featured the new morsels. You see I didn't really like the taste of them so kept rejecting recipes that used them. They were made with green and red nonpareils enrobing the creamy chocolate. Since the project objective – promote these new Merry Morsels® – hadn't been clearly communicated, I just left them out.

We hurried back to the test kitchens. Now, we started over, facing tremendous pressure and tight deadlines which the team wouldn't have had to endure if the communication hadn't been so poor. I hadn't clarified or checked in often enough and my boss hadn't communicated a clear goal in the first place.

We did get the cookbook into publishing in time, but sadly the Merry Morsels® didn't last more than one holiday season on the shelf. Maybe there weren't enough relevant recipes after all or it's possible that the Merry Morsels® actually didn't taste good enough in the first place. We will never know.

Vision First

For communication to work on any level, it is important to establish the overall goal and vision. What is the team/company/group trying to accomplish? Karen Connelly, Associate Vice President of Allergan, put it very succinctly, "You may not know HOW you are going to get there, but you do have to know WHERE you are going. Without a clear purpose or vision, leadership falls flat."

The vision must be very clear and easy to communicate. If it is clear, each stakeholder will understand the destination and can get passionate about the journey. If it isn't clear, then the team will be less motivated, less effective and ultimately less likely to achieve it.

Technology Does Not Mean the Rules of Communication are Suspended

Communicating in the age of high tech can present some unique challenges. Just as texting makes it hard to communicate emotion, the plethora of technology may make it hard to incorporate some simple interpersonal skills.

According to Dr. Loretta Malandro, author of the book *Speak Up, Show Up, and Stand Out*, becoming a powerful communicator is possible by following some commonsense rules including:

Create Positive Partnerships - Stop Negative Talk

Instead of tearing people down, build them up. When you hear employees and customers complaining about something, there's probably a reason for it. Check it out, but don't dwell on the negative.

Commit or Not - Don't Hedge

Be known as someone who communicates in a forthright, honest, and straightforward way. While you don't want to be cruel, you'll be far more effective when you tell it like it is instead of beating around the bush and equivocating for fear of hurting someone's feelings. Be firm but fair in the assessment of any given situation.

Own the Problem - Don't Blame or Make Excuses

Instead of looking for someone to blame for mistakes or problems, focus on looking for solutions and positive outcomes. As a leader, the buck stops on your desk.

Recover Quickly - Come Back Stronger

We are human—we all make mistakes and it's a given in life and in business. Acknowledge mistakes, learn from them, then bounce back and try again. Own it if the mistake happened because you did not communicate clearly.

Resilience is a theme we'll talk more about because bouncing back is another critical leadership attribute.

Communication Downside

While it is wonderful when communication works, it can be awful when it does not work. I was part of a hair care specialty brand that was planning to launch a line of all-natural products. That brand was run by someone who was very insecure in his position. He was not willing to admit when things weren't going right. He had more than an inkling that his product launch would not be well received, and he had plenty of advance warning that things were not right with the formulation.

Still, he communicated to his team that everything was on track, created samples for the product, created selling information, and had the sales force sell the products to retailers, creating space for them on the shelf.

The problem was, when the people who were working on the Research and Development (R&D) and Packaging communicated concerns to him, he blocked them. He told them they were being too negative, not willing to take risks, and wouldn't let that communication get back to the team. It's a fine balance between pragmatism and optimism.

Negativity isn't necessarily beneficial, but honesty is. He made no attempt to hear what was behind the negative issues and concern and missed a huge red flag. Retailers were expecting the product and, just two weeks before the product was supposed to ship, the formula still wasn't stable. The entire brand suffered as a result and the launch was cancelled.

The brand today no longer exists because the retailers were jaded. They were angry that they had been promised something and it never came. Not only didn't it come, but because the focus had been on those natural ingredients, there were no other new initiatives planned for the business so there was no news at all for the next 2 years. Hair care or beauty with no news? It was no surprise that the business tanked.

This shouldn't have been a surprise to anyone, but it was, all due to poor communication. Weak or dishonest communication often comes from a place of insecurity. An insecure leader does not want to give bad news because he is afraid it will reflect poorly on him. In the end, the situation reflected negatively on everyone. It is far better to communicate the issues clearly and get the team involved in solving them.

Communicating at All Levels

If a leader is communicating well with the team, but team members are not communicating well with each other, there can still be chaos. This is also true when the leader is not communicating well with upper management.

All levels need clear and effective messaging. Create cohesive, understandable, actionable and honest information sharing up, down and laterally.

Good communication means clear communication:

- A clear vision
- A shared roadmap
- Lots of check-in points
- Honesty
- Effective listening

Leaders must model and encourage this behavior by checking in often and reinforcing the value of communication. No one wants to end up with the childhood game of telephone, where the end message bears no resemblance to the original one. This is not the kind of following a leader needs or wants.

No Good Leadership Without Good Communication

I read an article recently in Forbes by global leadership expert Mike Myatt. He just comes right out and says: "It is simply impossible to become a great leader without being a great communicator." He points out that academia emphasizes things like enunciation and clear diction as being necessary to good communication.

According to Myatt, one of the most important communication skills is awareness of both internal and external forces, and an awareness of how communication is being handled, understood and acted on.

"I don't believe it comes as any great surprise that most leaders spend the overwhelming majority of their time each day in some type of an interpersonal situation. I also don't believe it comes as a great shock that a large number of organizational problems occur as a result of poor communications. It is precisely this paradox that underscores the need for leaders to focus on becoming great communicators," said Myatt.

In his article, Myatt goes on to outline what he feels are the most important aspects of communication for a leader and how good communication should also motivate action.

1. **Get specific:** Simple and concise is always better than complicated and confusing. Your goal is to weed out the superfluous and to make your words count.

2. **Focus on the leave-behinds not the take-aways:** The best communicators are not only skilled at learning and gathering information while communicating; they are also adept at transferring ideas, aligning expectations, inspiring action, and spreading their vision. Focus on the other party's wants, needs and desires. You'll learn far more than you ever would by focusing on your agenda.

3. **Have an open mind:** A leader takes their game to a whole new level the minute they willingly seek out those who hold dissenting opinions and opposing positions with the goal not of convincing them to change their minds, but with the goal of understanding what's on their mind.

4. **Read between the lines:** Take a moment and reflect back on any great leader that comes to mind... you'll find they are very adept at reading between the lines. They have the uncanny ability to understand what is not said or heard.

5. **When you speak, know what you're talking about:** Develop a technical command over your subject matter. If you don't possess subject matter expertise, few people will give you the time of day.

6. **Speak to groups as individuals:** Leaders don't always have the luxury of speaking to individuals in an intimate setting. Great communicators can tailor a message such that they can speak to 10 people in a conference room or 10,000 people in an auditorium and have them feel as if they were speaking directly to each one of them as an individual.

Making people feel like individuals, even in a crowd, is a magical skill. I've been in a room of 15,000 when I swore that a speaker was talking just to me. This happened twice, with Bill Clinton and Colin Powell. Both were able to accomplish this feat with mastery that locked in my attention. Whether you agree with their politics or not, it's hard to deny their powers of persuasion. While they are unique speakers and leaders, this ability is clearly one worth developing in order to become a leader that others would gladly follow.

Leveraging Leadership Concepts – So What Now?

1. Could you articulate the vision and roadmap for your current company or organization?
    a. Write it down and ask others to review it with you; make this request to the highest level you can.
    b. Keep it front and center at your desk.

2. When you must give difficult news, check your negativity. Lead with a possible solution.

3. Practice. Send a message you believe is clear, and then confirm it was well understood; did the message come across exactly as you'd intended? Confirm understanding or you'll end up with a useless holiday cookbook.

HUMILITY AND RESILIENCE, GUARANTEED TO INSPIRE

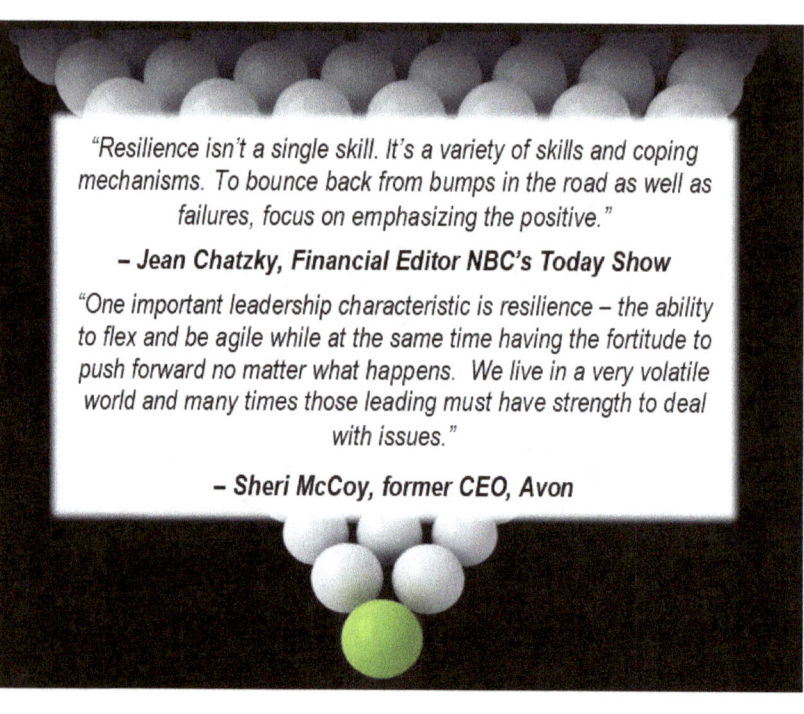

"Resilience isn't a single skill. It's a variety of skills and coping mechanisms. To bounce back from bumps in the road as well as failures, focus on emphasizing the positive."

– Jean Chatzky, Financial Editor NBC's Today Show

"One important leadership characteristic is resilience – the ability to flex and be agile while at the same time having the fortitude to push forward no matter what happens. We live in a very volatile world and many times those leading must have strength to deal with issues."

– Sheri McCoy, former CEO, Avon

CHAPTER SEVEN

HUMILITY AND RESILIENCE, GUARANTEED TO INSPIRE

While I have often had the privilege of sharing leadership moments with my team or even my clients, there have been many people over the course of my professional career that have shown me the way.

One of the first mentors to really spark innovative and resilient thinking in me was Doug Hall, the founder of the Eureka® Ranch in Cincinnati and of the Innovation Engineering Institute. He was a Procter and Gamble (P&G) marketer from the Boston area whose speech is always peppered with "wicked" and "awesome".

He has a contagious energy and charisma that made us want to be around him.

When Doug left P&G, he created this place where we could take our teams to go to generate new ideas: the Eureka® Mansion and then later the Eureka® Ranch. In the period of a couple of days, we would go from a brain dump of hundreds of ideas to a dozen completely written concepts ready to test. His process pulled out what was already in people's brains and broke down any pre-existing notions or assumptions. He fostered boundless thinking and free-speaking collaboration. I never walked out of one of his sessions without being inspired and without generating more than the number of ideas I had hoped to create.

Doug's method helped open minds to associative logic and to hidden connections. He gave us the blueprint on how to look through a different lens at a situation and come out with a positive solution. Quite often, a few days after I was at one of his sessions or at his ranch, I would come up with a big idea. The free flow of ideas didn't just stop when I was walking out of his building. Once my mind began operating in a productive and imaginative way, I could put things together that I hadn't put together that way before.

Doug deployed people he called trained brains. These were people trained to think differently and to nurture this ability in others. I was lucky enough to be trained by him to do this so I could go back to my company and spark innovation as if we were at the Eureka® Ranch. Since we couldn't always physically be there, the trained brains brought the culture and methods of innovation out to companies. I brought my trained brain back to New Jersey.

What Doug inspired in me is the expectation that even the toughest challenges can be solved. We just need to look at them a different way, ideally with a team of smart people. From working with Doug, I also realized that innovation and resilience could be taught; that imaginative and breakthrough thinking could be developed, as opposed to assuming this was an innate skill. While it may be true that some people are born with a natural ability to think big, everyone, and I mean everyone, can learn to do it.

The Need to Start Small

When you hear the word leadership, it is tempting to think that a leader always needs to be the top dog, commanding. However, one of the most important aspects of leadership is knowing when to command vs. when to sit back. It's important to be humble. A true leader knows how to bring out the best in the team. Unfortunately, many leaders lose sight of this and get caught up in the need to be the boss.

Sometimes when a leader attains the actual leadership title, power can cause him or her to become overly obsessed with having complete control in order to ensure certain outcomes. She might end up mistreating her team members purely as a means to an end.

Treating people in a high-handed way only ramps up their fears: fear of not hitting the targets set, fear of not getting a bonus, fear of getting fired.

When a team feels this way, positive and innovative approaches are stifled and the natural drive to think outside the box vanishes. The team cannot learn or grow.

Daniel Cable, in his book *Alive at Work – The Neuroscience of Helping Your People Love What They Do* tells the story of a UK food delivery service that was suffering from issues with their delivery of milk and bread to millions of consumers every day. Management had become increasingly metrics-driven in an effort to reduce costs and improve delivery times.

Each week, managers held weekly performance debriefs with their delivery drivers and went through a list of problems, complaints, and errors with a clipboard and pen.

Eventually, the drivers, many of whom had worked for the company for decades, became resentful. They wanted to foster rapport with their customers and build relationships that would lead to increased loyalty and sales. Management just didn't seem to value or respect the input of their seasoned employees.

This type of top-down leadership is outdated and counterproductive. By focusing only on control and the end outcomes, and not enough on their people, those leaders made it more difficult to achieve their own desired outcomes.

The key, then, is to help people feel purposeful, motivated, and energized so they can bring their best selves to work.

One of the ways to energize a team is to adopt the humble mindset of a servant-leader. Servant leaders view their key role as serving employees as they explore and grow, providing tangible and emotional support as the team works towards the goal.

"To put it bluntly, servant-leaders have the humility, courage, and insight to admit that they can benefit from the expertise of others who have less power than they do. They actively seek the ideas and unique contributions of the employees that they serve. This is how servant leaders create a culture of learning, and an atmosphere that encourages followers to become the very best they can," said Cable.

The concept of humility and servant leadership does not imply that leaders have low self-esteem. **On the contrary, servant leadership emphasizes that the responsibility of a leader is to increase the ownership, autonomy, and responsibility of followers—to encourage them to think for themselves and try their own ideas.**

In a recent meeting of volunteers, a local politician said she couldn't stand politicians but she felt that, "as a leader, she had to play this role to serve and she had to serve to feel fulfilled and engender the support of the entire county". "Asking what my constituents need and then doing it, that's what effective leadership is all about."

Here are a few pointers from Daniel Cable on how to achieve this type of leadership:

Ask how you can help employees do their own jobs better — then listen

It sounds deceptively simple: Rather than telling employees how to do their jobs better, start by asking them how you can help them do their jobs better. The effects of this approach can be powerful.

Consider the food-delivery business previously mentioned. After meeting with consultants at PricewaterhouseCoopers and some training, the management team tried a new format for its weekly performance meetings with the drivers. The new approach? Instead of nit-picking problems, each manager was trained to simply ask their drivers, "How can I help you deliver excellent service?" There was a lot of skepticism at first, as the drivers' dislike of managers was high, and trust was low. But as depot managers kept asking "How can I help you deliver excellent service?" some drivers started to offer suggestions. For example, one driver suggested new products like Gogurts® and string cheese that parents could get delivered early and pop into their kids' lunches before school. Another driver thought of a way to report stock shortages more quickly so that customers were not left without the groceries they ordered.

Continue to make small changes to create a virtuous cycle

As the drivers got credit for their ideas and saw them put into place, they grew more willing to offer more ideas, which made the depot managers more impressed and more respectful, which increased the delivery drivers' willingness to give ideas, and so on. This one simple change by management caused a positive outcome … simply by changing the behavior of managers from acting like the boss who already knows it all, to one who showed humility and caring.

Create low-risk spaces for employees to think of new ideas

Sometimes the best way for leaders to serve employees, and their organization, is to create a low-risk, safe space for employees to experiment with their ideas. By doing so, leaders encourage team members to push past the boundaries of what they already know. This can be a physical or virtual space, but it needs to be showcased and encouraged. It can mean allocating time, rewards or just a place to ideate.

Be humble

When leaders are humble, show respect, and ask how they can serve employees as they improve the organization, the outcomes can be outstanding. Perhaps equally important to increasing company results, is that servant leaders get to act like better human beings.

The Importance of Resilience and Not Living in the Past

Resilience is a concept that is important for both leaders and learners. It is the difference between the sapling that bends in the wind vs. the stagnant oak that gets blown down when a gust hits too hard. Resilience is the ability to handle whatever life throws at you. Having the elasticity to bend is an important part of true leadership.

Sheri McCoy, former CEO of Avon, told me that resilience and integrity top the list of the most important leadership qualities for her. "We live in a very volatile world and, as a leader, you need to acknowledge that there are things you can change and things you cannot."

Sheri talked about dealing with the situation when Avon was deluged with activist investors. This was clearly something she could not control. She needed the resilience to figure out a strategy for dealing with the situation, handling public opinion, and still being an inspiration to her team. She gracefully accepted their criticism, yet quickly bounced back.

One of my favorite quotes in this area is from a Bob Marley song. "You don't know how strong you are until being strong is the only choice you have." Cultivating resilience can mean you have the strength to deal with any situation.

Wendy Van Besien, a Leadership and Executive Coach, agrees that resilience is a top ten quality for any leader. "As a leader, you need to have the ability to overcome whatever adversity the team is facing, such as trauma, tragic events or everyday disturbances."

Alissa Hsu-Lynch, Board Member of the Honest Company and former VP, Johnson & Johnson Medical Devices, also agrees that resilience is a key quality needed for leadership. She puts a unique twist on it – she espouses resilience paired with learning agility. As A.I. emerges, resilience and the ability to adapt becomes even more essential.

"Leaders need the ability to respond to a rapidly changing marketplace and a high level of uncertainty globally. Political instability and the rapid pace of tech change make resilience and ability to learn paramount for leaders of all types".

In an article in Forbes entitled "7 Ways to Become a More Resilient Leader" Joseph Folkman, co-founder of leadership development firm Zenger Folkman, gives some helpful hints on how a new leader can develop this all-important quality. Folkman's team compared the most resilient leaders to the least on 37 behaviors and selected the top seven that showed the most significant difference. His list reflects many of the behaviors discussed in these chapters:

Communicate Powerfully

Some will often act individually and not inform others about what they are trying to do. When driving down the freeway, we appreciate it when people signal before they change lanes.

Signaling lets others know your intentions. The most resilient leaders are effective at communicating their intentions to others so they can pivot or bounce back quickly.

Act Humbly and Be Coachable

Resilient leaders are open to feedback and ask for it. They also demonstrate a real effort to improve. These leaders show up as both humble and coachable.

Build Positive/Trusting Relationships

Resilient leadership occurs when people can bring others along. By building trust and being open to differences, these leaders are able to create strong teams.

Take Bold Risks

Resilient leaders are not afraid to take risks and make bold changes.

Develop Others

The most resilient leaders were not only interested in their own development, but they are concerned about the development of others. Resiliency is needed when we encounter failure. Developing others helps everyone learn from their mistakes.

Champion Change

Resilient leaders are willing to change and are able to provide the leadership to ensure that the organization will also change. Change takes courage and requires a vision about where the organization is going. Resilient leaders embrace change, share a clear vision and encourage others to change.

Be Decisive

Making decisions is always difficult because no person has all the data or understands all eventualities. However, organizations cannot move forward until a decision gets made.

The most resilient leaders are effective at making decisions and moving forward. If they make the wrong decision, they are quick to move in another direction.

True Grit – How to Lead in Troubled Times

Along with resilience, strong leadership requires a dash of true grit. Grit is part courage and part conviction. Carla Vernón, former Corporate Officer at General Mills and now CEO at the Honest Co., listed courage as a much-needed quality for a good leader. "We are in a time when certainty is no longer assured, so to lead now means to make choices, decisive choices despite uncertainty, choices grounded on courage, bold actions that accept potential risk."

Grit is unerring passion and perseverance toward long-term goals. This concept became well known as a trait of successful people after a TED Talk given by Angela Duckworth that has been seen, to date, by over 18 million viewers.

In it, she argues that talent and intelligence are inferior predictors of success when compared to grit. This is consistent with the marshmallow experiment too.

Duckworth decided to leave her career in management consulting and took up teaching 7th graders in the New York City School system. She began to notice that her strongest students were not necessarily the ones with the highest IQs.

They were the ones who had the grit to go the distance and do the work. Duckworth made yet another drastic career change. She went back to school to become a psychologist. "I started studying kids and adults in all kinds of super challenging settings and in every study my question was who is successful here and why?"

"My research team and I went to West Point Military Academy. We studied rookie teachers working in really tough neighborhoods asking which teachers are still going to be here teaching by the end of the year."

"In all those very different contexts one characteristic emerged as a significant predictor of success…it was grit. Grit is sticking with your future, day in, day out, not just for the week, not just for the month, but for years, and working really hard to make that future a reality. Grit is living life like it's a marathon, not a sprint.," said Duckworth.

The Grit Gap

It is one thing for a leader to have the grit needed to push on to victory, but how does one engender grit in the team at large? Overall, there is a glaring grit gap in organizations, according to Ben Fanning, author of the book "The Quit Alternative" and the article "7 Ways Top Leaders Develop Grit in Their Team" from Inc. Magazine.

According to Fanning, annual reviews cover things like leadership impact, effective communication, intelligent risk taking, and getting results, which are important aspects to measure, but he feels that they are incomplete. Fanning believes you can give your team a success boost by helping them to develop grit intentionally using the following steps:

1. **Explain the importance of grit:** Even if there is not a box to check in your team's annual review for grit, explain the importance of perseverance for the team members' long-term success. Start by showing Angela Duckworth's TED Talk on grit or having a conversation about how grit can be helpful in achieving long term goals.

2. **Track consistent progress:** Emphasize taking frequent small actions towards your team's big goals instead of cramming right before a big deadline. Deciding on a daily action plan that contributes to the longer goal allows easy tracking of the team's progress. This simple process helps ensure long-term team and individual continuity and avoids burnout.

3. **Frame failure as an opportunity for learning:** Instead of hiding mistakes or blaming others for failure, ask your team to talk about what they have learned. This pushes them to learn from their mistakes.

4. **Show your team how they already have grit:** Help your team identify a time when they have shown grit. Ask your team to think of a tough experience they got through. This proves they can persevere, and it lays the foundation for them to build upon in the future.

Leaders with Grit

My brother always comes to mind when I think of resilience and true grit. Jason Barnett inspires many. It is his application of grit that has seen him through many challenging times in his career. He would say that resilience and grit are equally important. "You need to be able to overcome failure or setbacks and the team needs to see leaders who move on and get past it. Leading by example in this area is a great way of passing along the concept of true grit."

After realizing that the public markets were not the most effective channel for generating value in the real estate industry, Jason and his leadership team sold the public company and started over again. They had the grit to start over to capitalize the company in a new way. They courageously built a new and thriving portfolio of commercial real estate that is even larger than its predecessor. They couldn't have done this without grit and resilience.

Jason's company demonstrated a compelling resilience as they reimagined their future. Many of their team followed them right into their next venture. Demonstrating humility while leveraging the power of resiliency can only improve the chances that you will be the leader everyone wants to follow.

Leveraging Leadership Concepts – So What Now?

1. Advocate and honor resilience – be sure to frame failures as a learning opportunity.

2. Watch the Angela Duckworth TED Talk with your team. Discuss how it applies.

3. Teach and instill grit – think, articulate, and track progress toward both long-term goals and short-term milestones.

4. Servant leadership and humility can inspire teams and establish leadership priorities. This is easily begun through a volunteer activity. Serve others – nothing makes you more humble.

PINK LEADERSHIP

Cracking the Glass Ceiling

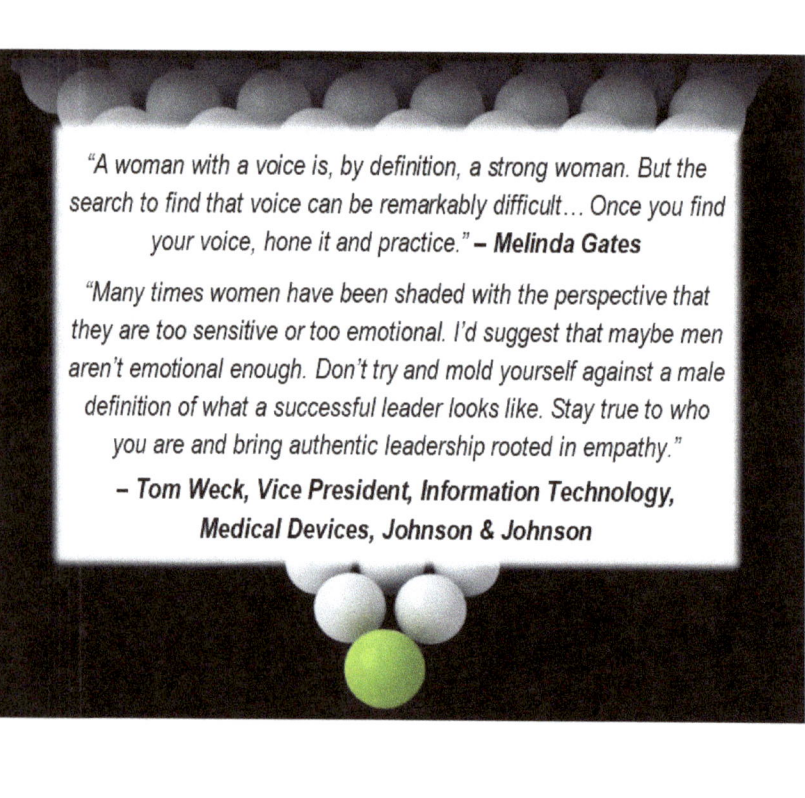

"A woman with a voice is, by definition, a strong woman. But the search to find that voice can be remarkably difficult… Once you find your voice, hone it and practice." *– Melinda Gates*

"Many times women have been shaded with the perspective that they are too sensitive or too emotional. I'd suggest that maybe men aren't emotional enough. Don't try and mold yourself against a male definition of what a successful leader looks like. Stay true to who you are and bring authentic leadership rooted in empathy."

– Tom Weck, Vice President, Information Technology, Medical Devices, Johnson & Johnson

CHAPTER EIGHT

PINK LEADERSHIP

Cracking the Glass Ceiling

I t was only in the mid-20th century that women began to be considered at the forefront of the business world. It began with World War II, when women had to go into jobs traditionally held by men, because the men were all overseas fighting.

Posters of Rosie the Riveter promoted the fact that women were needed in all types of jobs traditionally held by men. Being true patriots, women heeded the call and went to work in factories and in companies.

However, when the war ended and men reclaimed their jobs, many women were disappointed to return to the kitchen.

Over the next few decades, women continued to fight for positions beyond the traditional female roles. It has taken decades to enable a cultural acceptance of women in leadership roles outside the home and the battle is still being waged in many parts of the world today. This cultural bias has helped contribute to the slow pace of women advancing in business.

Remember the story about my early days at J&J, when I had the opportunity to proactively attract new moms to my business? I looked at the entire male-dominated department and knew I had to invite new parents back to my team.

I wanted their knowledge on my business. New moms understood the target consumer, so it was great for the business and coincidentally qualified me as a trailblazer for recruiting them. Women with babies became sought-after marketers.

Defining the Glass Ceiling

If you look this phrase up in Wikipedia, the definition of a glass ceiling is a "metaphor used to represent an invisible barrier that keeps a given demographic from rising beyond a certain level in a hierarchy."

It has been 100 years since the equal rights amendment was passed; yet we still have to study and discuss how women can break the glass ceiling. Women make up half the world's population, and an increasing number of women are entering the workforce every year.

In countries like Japan, the domestic burden still falls mostly on their shoulders, even when they work outside the home.

In spite of the discussions about diversity and inclusion in organizations, women in leadership roles are still the minority. They have fewer opportunities than their male counterparts to showcase their full potential, and they must work harder to prove themselves repeatedly as they work their way up to senior positions.

Over the history of my career, I've observed pretty consistently that woman usually had to be overqualified for a leadership position in order to get it. Concurrently, men often were placed into a promotion almost prematurely. A male counterpart could have only a limited number of the skills listed for the position and still win the role.

They often moved up based as much on their bravado as on their experience or proven track record. Men were then allowed to grow into the full position. Women often had to prove their readiness first. We had to demonstrate success in a position before it was officially awarded. I always took this as a signal to do more in my current role. Perhaps it was unfair, but it was the reality.

Nora Frenkiel, an activist and writer, first coined the term glass ceiling in 1984, and 35 years later not enough progress has been made. In 1995, there were no women serving as CEOs of Fortune 500 companies, and only 10 percent served as Board members. By 2025, women made up just 11 percent of Fortune 500 CEOs and women's boardroom participation remains under 34 percent.

Yet more than half of all managerial and professional occupations in the U.S. are held by women today. Firms with more women in the C-suite are more profitable than those without. New laws began to force an increase in the percentage of women on Boards, but it has taken legislation to enable this. While the world is evolving, women are still lagging behind when it comes to leadership roles in business.

With women still pushing to reach the top, they are faced with a range of challenges that many of their male counterparts may not understand. It is these issues that are holding back many women from achieving their goal of becoming leaders at their companies.

As more efforts to recruit and develop women emerge, the elimination of biases is being placed at the forefront of public discussion. Many studies have identified the following as the best ways for women to break the glass ceiling.

Understand the Confidence Gap

A study by Washington State University psychologist, Joyce Ehrlinger, and Cornell psychologist, David Dunning, found that men overestimate their abilities and performance while women underestimate both. In reality, the quality of their performances does not differ. This confidence gap is alarming given the growing body of evidence that shows just how devastating lack of confidence can be. **Success, it turns out, correlates just as closely with confidence as it does with actual competence.**

Virginia M. Rometty, President and CEO of IBM and the first woman to head the company, told this story from early in her career. She was offered a top position but felt she did not have enough experience. She was asked if she wanted the job and then told the recruiter she needed time to think about it and would give him an answer the next day.

That night, her husband asked her, "'Do you think a man would have ever answered that question that way?" Rometty said, "What it taught me was you have to be very confident, even though you're so self-critical inside."

Don't Negotiate Like a Man – Negotiate Like a Woman

Linda Babcock, a professor of economics at Carnegie Mellon University and the author of Women Don't Ask, has found male business school students initiate salary negotiations four times as often as female students do. When women do negotiate, they ask for 30 percent less money than men do.

Researchers have found that women may be avoiding negotiations because they perceive that there is a social cost to be paid for engaging in these types of interactions. Rightfully so, as women are penalized more than men for initiating negotiations. How does a woman successfully advocate for herself given the associated risks? Make it about the role or the business, not yourself.

After receiving her first job offer from Facebook, Sheryl Sandberg tells the following story. "I went back to Mark and said I couldn't accept. I told him, of course you realize that you're hiring me to run your deal team, so you want me to be a good negotiator. This is the only time you and I will ever be on opposite sides of the table." Sandberg negotiated effectively by connecting what was good for her with what was good for the company.

Get Comfortable with Rejection

While women begin their careers with ambitions that are just as high, if not slightly higher than their male peers, most eventually scale back their goals and become less likely to pursue promotions, job transfers, and high-profile assignments. Many assume this is because women are more risk averse or have career preferences that differ from their male colleagues. Some think it's the impact of wanting more time with their children. Raina Brands and Isabel Fernandez-Mateo of the London Business School conducted a study that points to a much subtler reason.

The study of more than 10,000 senior executives in the U.K. found that women were much less likely to apply for a job if they had been rejected for a similar job in the past. Men were also less likely to apply if they had been rejected, but the effect was much stronger for women, more than 1.5 times as strong.

The takeaway for employers and policy makers is that while encouraging more women to throw their hat into the ring is worthwhile, it is even more valuable to ensure that recruiting and promotion processes are indeed fair, objective and transparent. Women need to see rejection as a chance for progress and courage, rather than a reflection of personal value. Never been rejected? Maybe you should be aiming higher.

Anna Wintour, historic Editor-in-Chief of Vogue, was originally rejected by the very industry she now runs. After just nine months as Junior Fashion Editor, Wintour was fired from Harper's Bazaar for being too edgy. At a fashion industry conference in New York, she told the audience, "I recommend that you all get fired. It's a great learning experience."

The Importance of Role Models

No one can argue with the assertion that having a role model makes learning and advancing at work a whole lot easier. However, when it comes to female leadership models, it becomes a catch 22 question. Where do we find women that can act as role models? How do you encourage women to become role models and what does that mean?

A study published in the Journal of Experimental Social Psychology shows exactly how role models are an incredibly effective way to encourage women to make different choices. The effect is based on the concept that seeing is believing, and it works on multiple levels.

The first level is inspiration

When women see other women in leadership roles, they find it easier to see themselves in such roles and are more likely to put themselves forward. The study showed that female students were more likely to choose a major in STEM (science, technology, engineering, and math – a typically male-dominated area) when they were assigned a female professor. The study also showed that retention of junior-level female employees is highly correlated with the number of female supervisors.

The second level is acknowledgement

Men can see women in leadership roles and make that mental turn around the corner where they acknowledge that a woman can do the job. It makes it easier to break the glass ceiling if males in the company are not actively trying to discourage such advancement.

In summary, the study found the following:

- Exposure to female role models empowered women's behavior and self-evaluations.

- Exposure to female role models eliminated the gender performance gap.

One of my role models has been Sharon D'Agostino (formerly Global President of two Johnson & Johnson consumer franchises and Vice President of Corporate Citizenship for the corporation). She offers great advice for women wanting to create a plan for their career that includes a leadership role. Sharon suggests that each woman needs to assess the environment where she is and adapt her plan. If women are in the extreme minority, that is often a difficult place to be. However, her advice has worked for me in diverse companies and cultures:

- **Be yourself:** Don't try to mimic the dominant leadership style but understand it. Find ways that you can lead as yourself without having to compromise who you are as a person.

- **Speak up and speak out:** Establish your point of view, don't be shy (meetings, email, let people know what you think) and make it matter.

- **Step up:** Accept opportunities to take on different responsibilities and roles, volunteer to do things to show you can stretch, but don't sacrifice your life balance.

- **Demonstrate your strengths/skills:** Find ways to demonstrate your strengths in whatever role you take on.

- **Know your business and demonstrate that you do:** Know your facts/organization/consumer, etc. Be certain to share this knowledge whenever appropriate.

- **Ask questions:** Do this so you both understand the situation and demonstrate your eagerness to learn.

Dealing with a Double Standard

Bill McComb is the beloved former boss of mine who talked with me about nurturing female leadership in his many roles. He taught it, modeled it and stood up for women throughout his career as Deputy Company Group Chairman Orthopedics and Neurologic Devices at J&J, CEO of Liz Claiborne/Kate Spade and as a member on several Boards.

According to Bill, the status of women in leadership is better in the U.S. than anywhere else but still not equal. "The reality is that women are held to different standards, and some of the toughest critics of women are other women. A strong woman faces risks that a strong man doesn't. I think that women, more than men, have to be connectors – they tend to be more gifted and forge individual bonds with more people than the average guy does."

"Men can be demonstratively strong and courageous while it's assumed that women have to have strong relationships to work through patriarchal cultures. It's 2019 and I can't believe how ridiculously low representation numbers are on Boards and at top of companies. I cannot believe that there now has to be a law to get women into the leadership roles they have always deserved."

Another favorite manager of mine, Owen Rankin, was known for mentoring and promoting women. When asked if he sees unique challenges for women, he said, "The one big challenge that I see with women leaders is around humility. Humility can sometimes be seen as a weakness. For my team, I always concentrate on building up women's confidence. I remind them that their styles often drive great outcomes. I also work on getting them to be less tentative."

He goes on to say, "It can be hard for women to seem both strong and humble, but it can be equally hard for women to show up as strong without being too arrogant. There's a broader tolerance for how men behave as leaders than for women. While it may actually be difficult for men to embrace humility and servant leadership, it's important. We need to have conversations about how women can be leaders and drivers of success even if uncomfortable. It may not feel right the first few times you try it."

Sheri McCoy looked at male vs. female advancement and even today, she sees a culture where "it's tough for women to find the answer. Strength in women is often seen as arrogant or aggressive. Other leaders and the women themselves don't always see or appreciate their inner strength."

How to Shatter the Glass Ceiling

In a posting on hubspot.com, Katie Burke shares tips to help women shatter the glass ceiling. A few influential suggestions of hers are to:

Recognize that success is plentiful: Some women are convinced that there is a finite amount of power and achievement in the world. The truth is that power and success are not limited resources. When women advance, it is rarely at the expense of men (or other women).

Aim high: While men usually dream big, women tend to have more modest goals. Women should be encouraged to express ambition. Everyone should stretch their imaginations about the role of women in the workplace, and females should be empowered to strive for executive leadership roles.

Build a network: Busy women, who often have caretaking responsibilities in addition to careers, tend to avoid after-hours networking events and extracurriculars. Networking events should be prioritized in order to foster personal growth. Set a goal to make 10 new connections every few months.

Toot your own horn: Women traditionally downplay their accomplishments. Toss humility aside and boast about triumphs. Women should create online portfolios, publish blogs and/or update their LinkedIn profiles.

Let go of perfection: Having it all is an elusive myth. Instead of striving for perfection in all areas, women should aim for growth in what matters most. This can be personal or professional and will morph over time.

Mari Baker also offered wisdom for women seeking the leadership track. She echoes Sharon's advice to step up and speak up. She advocates getting out and being seen, joining in with a group that's going out and creating the opportunity yourself if you don't get invited.

She recalls asking important people she admired to be her mentors and capitalizing on any few minutes of facetime she could get with senior management, no matter how short. Mari counsels, "Don't be afraid to raise your hand – Speak up, make a positive impression and show how awesome you are. Remind people that there's value in having you in the room."

Karen Connelly, Associate Vice President, Learning and Development for Allergan, has trained hundreds of marketing and sales leaders. In her opinion, one of the challenges today in developing successful leaders is the need for authenticity.

"Leadership in the workplace used to look more stoic. Today, feelings are more out there in a positive way. This takes expressing a certain amount of vulnerability that can still be hard for women to demonstrate."

In her view, female leaders have to share their true colors. "Men can see vulnerability as a stereotypical feature of less strong leaders, but this is no longer the case.

The first step to leadership is knowing who you are: through values and experiences. Try some sort of exercise to understand yourself (e.g. StrengthsFinder, a value cards exercise, insights/colors for communications). It doesn't matter how you measure it, but you have to know your values before inspiring others."

Carla Vernón, Natural & Organic Operating Unit President and Corporate Officer at General Mills takes it one step further. "My thoughts, specific to women leaders and women of diverse ethnicities, are these – work together even outside of the immediate context and have a strategy to visibly and vocally be a united force for each other. Women need to intentionally work together to use our power to support each other. Amplify what the other person said, give positive feedback in the actual moment."

The Direct Approach

Danika Laszuk was Vice President of Marketing at Jawbone when she shared this story. "Years ago, I had just started a new job, and during my first meeting with the engineering team, the director of the team called me a little girl. He said it with a smile on his face, and in a joking tone, but it still mortified me (and shut me up) in this room of men with whom I'd be working very closely over the next few years. Rather than going bananas in the moment, I followed him to his office after the meeting and told him I wasn't ok with him talking to me like that and undermining me with the team before I'd even had a chance to meet everyone.

He assured me he was kidding around, and apologized, and then said it was cool that I stood up for myself like that. He said that if I wasn't afraid to stand up to him in that way, then he knew I would fight for my ideas and for the team. I know he was surprised that I reacted so strongly to his joke, but he respected me for speaking up, and we went on to have a great relationship."

The bottom line is this - it's still really difficult to be a successful woman in business. You may have to work harder, deal with bias, and push yourself, but it can be done. With confidence, strength, and empathy, make yourself known and demonstrate your value.

Negotiate when you have to and stand firm where you can. Follow that path to find your voice but expect it to be hard. Smart, motivated women are accustomed to facing challenges.

I truly thought that by 2025 we would no longer need these conversations, but we do. As we succeed, it is our mandate to pull other women up with us. By 2030, I hope that female leadership will simply be leadership and we can be the leaders everyone follows without having to reference our gender.

Leveraging Leadership Concepts – So What Now?

1. Practice speaking up. Say at least one thing of value in every major meeting.

2. While it is not fair, it is still true that women leaders may have to try harder and prove more before they're recognized. Identify two of your recent achievements and be sure they're well known.

3. Join a women's group or affinity group to become a unified force of good. Voice your support of other women and minority populations publicly whenever the opportunity arises. Build your own network.

TRUE LEADERS ARE ALWAYS LEARNING (AND TEACHING)

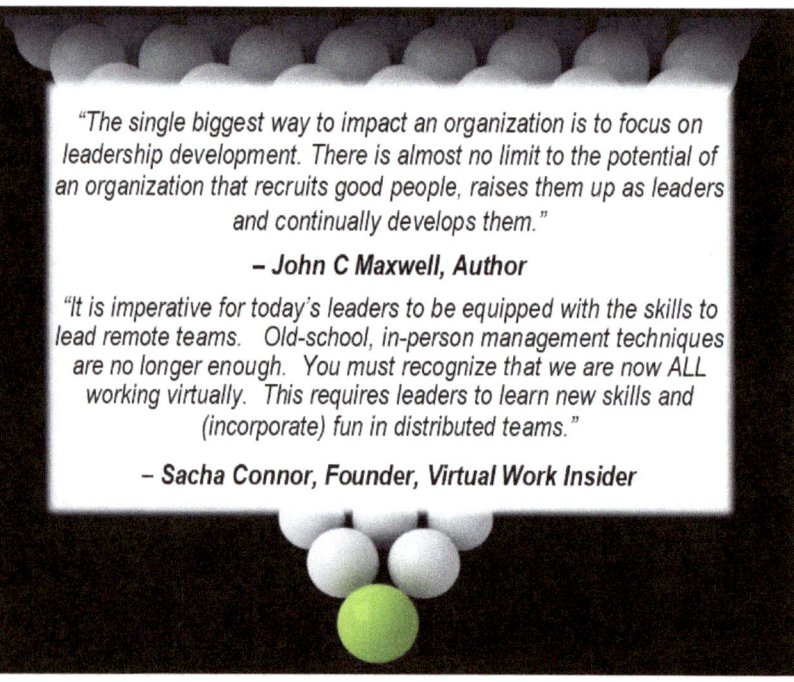

"The single biggest way to impact an organization is to focus on leadership development. There is almost no limit to the potential of an organization that recruits good people, raises them up as leaders and continually develops them."

– John C Maxwell, Author

"It is imperative for today's leaders to be equipped with the skills to lead remote teams. Old-school, in-person management techniques are no longer enough. You must recognize that we are now ALL working virtually. This requires leaders to learn new skills and (incorporate) fun in distributed teams."

– Sacha Connor, Founder, Virtual Work Insider

TRUE LEADERS ARE ALWAYS LEARNING (AND TEACHING)

I have observed that the best leaders are intellectually curious, which means they are always in learning mode. This is usually because they realize they do not know everything and are eager to learn more.

They seek to learn better leadership and management practices, but also a better understanding of their industry, their customers, opportunities, and more. If you don't have that constant intellectual curiosity and aren't willing to acknowledge that you don't know everything, it will be hard to become a good leader.

One example from my own experience, recently, involves developing a deep digital expertise. I ran a marketing agency with an amazing team. While we could handle any integrated marketing communication or digital challenge, we were not all digital natives. Some of us are over 40, so the immediate assumption by clients had been that we may not know what we're talking about when it comes to digital marketing.

This has meant that we have often all had to demonstrate what we've learned on digital and social marketing, as we apply it in the unique situations presented to us by our clients. We may have to show more expertise than millennials, which means being open to constant learning.

I decided that I wanted to amp up my skills and learn more. I was offered an opportunity to select the class that I would teach at NYU in marketing.

I chose a class on integrated marketing communications because I knew it would force me to become an expert.

I eagerly pushed myself to develop a rich curriculum on integrated marketing communications (I was going to teach it to a class filled with global master's degree students) and mastery was crucial. In order to teach, you certainly need to understand. However, even if you're not going to teach and you're planning to lead a project, you also need to establish your credibility.

Researching, taking classes and then developing a class and its materials was a very productive way for me to become a leader in digital marketing strategy and execution. I may not actually execute tactics, but I'd put my digital strategy recommendations up against anyone's. This would not have been possible without a commitment to learning.

Fostering Intellectual Curiosity

One of the best ways to encourage the next generation of leaders is to foster intellectual curiosity. All too often, the regular education system creates students who follow orders, rather than curious individuals who want to continue learning.

Sheri McCoy, former CEO of Avon, says that "environment trumps everything." She believes it is important for an organization to create an environment where intellectual curiosity is valued, and people feel safe to explore.

Having worked with her, I know she is phenomenal at creating this kind of learning culture. In speaking about her own journey, she said "It is important to try new things, as we may not have a straightforward linear career.

Experiential learning is also important, especially when it comes to being attuned to the digital world. Study it (social media), be more thoughtful, think about what your mother would say if she saw all those things out there."

Sheri offered that the worst leaders are the ones who have their own agenda and are only concerned with protecting their turf instead of growing the next generation of leaders. "They protect themselves at the peril of the people who work for them. Good leaders engender an environment where curiosity is valued and cultivated to encourage people to learn." One of her favorite quotes is from JFK when he states that leadership and learning are indispensable to one another.

Learn on Your Own

One of the most important things that I did to develop my team was to work to expand their horizons. I hoped to teach them something new while they teach me just as much. I asked them to go out and learn and share their newfound knowledge with the rest of us.

They were encouraged to take classes on any topic of their choice, every year. They cover a wide range of seminars that may or may not have immediate relevance for their work today. If they believe it enhances their thinking in any way, their only obligation is to take notes and share a summary with the rest of the team.

I also take several classes and attend conferences every year. There's always so much to learn that choosing which event to attend or what classes to take is daunting. One year, I went to the Toy Fair. Last year included a visit to the Firehouse Expo and a Procter & Gamble Alumni Reunion and Training event. I recently took a series of webinars on new digital metrics and another on the emerging ecosystem around the cannabis industry. At the same time, I teach webinars on consumer connectedness and emerging technology. I never know where the next kernel of knowledge is going to come from, but I'm always looking.

Mari Baker is a huge proponent of self-responsibility when it comes to learning about leadership. "If you are an emerging leader, you have to be dedicated to learning on your own, even if the company you work for does not provide active access to learning. There are so many resources, from books to YouTube videos, that provide access to learning on every subject under the sun. People need to recognize that they cannot just sit back and have the organization they work for provide a leadership track."

Teach Good Leadership Skills Through Modeling and Mentoring

Modeling good leadership skills and specifically mentoring team members is a valuable way for people to gain leadership skills. Mentoring not only helps others but inevitably you learn as much from your mentee as she does from you. I find this today as I lean on interns to educate me about podcast production and artificial intelligence, social media and much more.

First, I considered it my responsibility (and privilege) to mentor my own Luminations team unofficially and as many students of marketing as I can. Second, I take on several official mentoring roles each year. Of course, there's never enough time to mentor everyone who seeks advice. As with all my endeavors, I believe I can always improve as a mentor and am currently working toward fewer mentees with whom I can offer a greater time-commitment.

I have spoken about my J&J mentors before and Sharon D'Agostino was one of them. She had a way of making people believe in their potential and their possibilities. She instilled confidence so that we believed we could achieve something even if we'd never done it before.

The bottom line was that we always wanted to give 110% when working with Sharon. We knew that her expectation was that we would always bring our best effort and ideas. Great mentors not only offer support in challenging times, but also make us want to impress them. Her high hopes came from a place of believing in us, not tearing us down; pulling us up to drive our business forward.

Ultimately, Sharon became the Vice President of Corporate Giving for Johnson & Johnson. She went beyond the endless possibilities of building the business to the endless possibilities of healing the world. She worked to make life better for women and children around the globe. To know that the company selected her for that role was also inspiring.

Many people wanted to follow her there. What is better than to give away millions a year for causes that are important? She is a prime illustration of how great leaders make us want to be our best, not out of fear but out of pride.

Leaders must be willing to stand up for their teams and break down barriers for them. Owen Rankin, who was President of the Johnson's Baby Company when I worked for him, was a senior leader who created an environment to help his team do its best. He shielded us from all the politics that could hamper our efforts. He saw his job as paving the way for us to get our job done in an effective and powerful way.

Owen was one of my first managers who really preached giving our best efforts both to work and family. He actually walked the talk. He coached his kids in soccer and made time for everybody on his team at work. He expected other people to do the same: make their families a priority as well as their work and not be ashamed to do so.

Family time used to be something that we snuck away to do and didn't put on our calendars. If we left for a school play, a Halloween parade, or a child's dentist appointment, it was a secret. It was seen as a potential lack of work focus.

Working for Owen, this was no longer a risk. It was part of our identity and something he wanted to cultivate as much as our professional strengths.

He is one of my role models when it comes to leadership. He says humbly, "I feel a lot smarter about good leadership now that I look back over the past 40 years. However, I would have gotten to a better place sooner if I had had someone to help me understand what good leadership looks like. If I saw earlier the core aspects of what good leaders do, and if I had understood that you can lead from the top, middle or bottom, I would have gotten to the good leadership rung much sooner."

Jim Chambers was my CEO at Netgrocer when I first started. He acknowledged my skills as a marketer and gave me the freedom to structure my team. He was a team builder, effective collaborator, and had a great sense of humor. He is the one who taught me to lighten up a little bit – even though he worked very, very, hard, many days a week, he never missed a chance to make us laugh. Jim trusted and leaned on his team and made us all feel important.

His sense of humor made even the most difficult days survivable. Watching Jim nurture a fledging technology company and prepare to take it public was a great training ground for me.

I could see how he operated, how he honored the experts on his team and how he put his people first at all times. Today he is chairman of the TIAA Board. His example of leadership and his mentorship allowed me to position myself to step into his shoes when he left the company.

Leadership Learners

If you think about leaders like Elon Musk, you are reminded of the fact that he was not afraid of huge challenges in areas that he did not understand. While a controversial figure, he bravely pursued battery power, space, and underground tunneling just to name a few.

He had to learn a lot about them to do it and had to surround himself with experts in order to make it happen at Tesla. While he has made blunders, he is clearly a lifelong learner turning intellectual curiosity into a successful company.

In the past, General Electric was known as having unparalleled management and leadership training. They had formal classes that everybody at every level was encouraged to take. Learning was not seen as missing work; it was presented as a privilege and an honor while still being mandatory.

Over the years, I experienced state-of-the-art leadership development programs at companies such as Johnson & Johnson and Procter and Gamble. In particular, at Johnson & Johnson, 30 percent of my rating as a manager at review time was linked to how I was developing talent that reported to me.

Other unique programs included one at Colgate Palmolive, a comprehensive rotational program where marketers also rotated through Finance and Supply Chain/Manufacturing and Regulatory. Those experiences can be very valuable as part of cross-functional training and development.

At Procter and Gamble, I rotated into Sales, as did all marketers. Calling on retailers made me a much better marketer. This meant they were training good leaders, ones who had an understanding of many of the key functions of the company, not just their own area.

However, as budgets have gotten tighter and training has ostensibly become less of a priority, these programs have begun to fade. Sadly, as many programs do not appear to have an immediate positive impact on the business or the bottom line, it is hard to attribute the growth of talent to the financial strength of a company; so, these programs have begun to be trimmed.

Scaling back on learning means that many companies have failed to nurture the kind of leadership they would like to have. They are not spending enough resources encouraging people to learn, and they are not investing enough time and money in talent development. This is a short-term focus that can starve their ability to grow leadership talent for the future. So, make sure to create your own development plan.

A Final Thought on Learning Leadership

At the end of the day, learning leadership is like learning any other skill. Beyond the basic knowledge of the subject, we must have a deep motivation to become a leader and the courage to act. I want the result of this book to be informed action that leads to positive development. I hope that lifelong learners will leverage their knowledge into true leadership.

Don't wait for someone to take you by the hand and nurture your leadership skills, although if this does happen, relish it. My hope is that you develop your own path and that you will be able to leverage the leadership concepts, counsel and stories from these pages. Take action and do some of the "So what now?" steps listed at the end of each chapter; start today… maybe right now.

Follow Happily

My favorite leaders have always been people with whom I want to be. I just wanted to be in their orbit, absorbing their mentorship and emulating their approaches. This is part of inspiring good leadership skills.

Creating a think-big, can-do culture takes talent to new places. We want to be with these influencers and to prove them right. In essence, they help us say "I can do it". They allow us to ask questions without feeling inadequate or weak. They break down barriers for us and tout our achievements, so we can remain humble. They encourage us to try our wings and help us recover when we fail.

Find the leader whose affection you want, whose orbit entices you, whose enthusiasm and passion ignites yours, and whose results and successes are abundant. Learn as much as you can so you too can become the leader that everyone wants to follow.

Leveraging Leadership Concepts – So What Now?

1. Evaluate yourself. Be honest and do it often.

2. Ask your colleagues and direct reports to assess your leadership across three key measures that you consider important in your organization.

3. If not rated highly on any of these, ask them what you can do today to get better.

4. Identify a mentor/role model and approach her/him. Become both a mentor and a mentee.

5. Stay positive and be grateful. Remember that it takes time to become the leader that everyone wants to follow.

STRATEGIC LEADERSHIP IN BUSINESS EXITS

Lessons in Letting Go

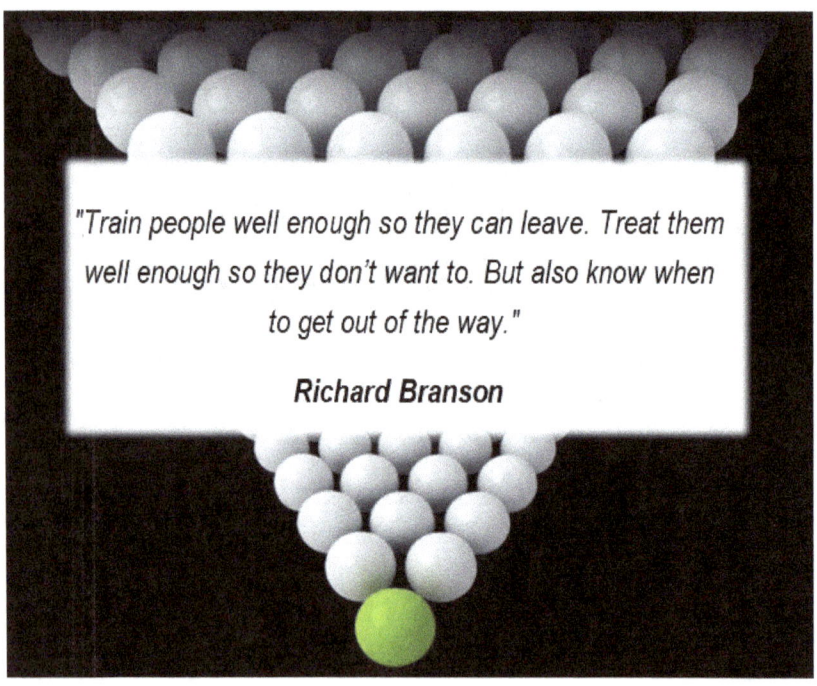

"Train people well enough so they can leave. Treat them well enough so they don't want to. But also know when to get out of the way."

Richard Branson

STRATEGIC LEADERSHIP IN BUSINESS EXITS

Lessons in Letting Go

There are moments in business that test you not just as a founder or executive, but as a human being. Selling the company you built from the ground up is one of those moments. It calls on every skill you've developed, every value you've upheld, and every ounce of perspective you've gathered along the way. It's the kind of decision that transcends spreadsheets and equity stakes. It touches your identity, your purpose, and the legacy you hoped to leave.

When I started Luminations, I was fueled by a sense of vision and purpose. I knew what I wanted to build: a values-driven, people-centered, high-performance company that delivered strategic marketing solutions while honoring the full humanity of those involved. I knew I wanted to build a business that stood for something, not just in the marketplace, but in the lives of the people it touched.

What I did not fully envision—what I don't think any entrepreneur truly does at the beginning—was the day I would step away from it. Like many builders, I was focused on creation, not completion. I had my head down, busy scaling, hiring, refining systems, attracting clients, and weathering storms. The idea of letting go felt abstract at best and premature at worst.

Over time, I came to realize a simple but profound truth: completion is part of every leader's journey. The best ones know that early. They lead not just for the now, but for the next phase as well. They build with succession in mind, whether the successor is family, internal leadership talent, or an acquiring company that shares their values.

Leadership, at its core, is not ownership. It is stewardship. It is about guiding something forward, preparing it for growth, and knowing when your role in that process has come to a natural close.

Leadership in the Midst of Crisis

The global pandemic was a crucible that tested every assumption we had about leadership, business strategy, and resilience. For me, it became a clarifying force in thinking about my company's future.

In the early, uncertain days of COVID-19, I realized quickly that leadership had to do much more than just providing direction, I had to help create stability. The world was changing rapidly—sometimes by the hour—and our people needed more than corporate strategies, they needed grounding. They needed reassurance that, even in the midst of chaos, we could find clarity and move forward with intention.

The noise was relentless. Daily headlines, shifting public health guidance, growing fear. There was no playbook. There was only presence and my best judgment.

In those moments, I asked myself—and my team—three fundamental questions:

1. What matters most right now?
2. What do we still control?
3. What must be let go?

These became our anchors. They helped us sift through to find clarity in confusion. In doing so, we became more than a company trying to survive a crisis—we became a community finding strength in shared purpose.

I also learned that in times of crisis, good leadership becomes even more deeply human. Connection supercedes control. My team didn't need me to have all the answers. They needed me to be present, transparent, and emotionally available. They needed to see that I wasn't hiding the hard truths—and that I believed we could face them together.

I made a deliberate choice to lead with transparency. I spoke openly about what I knew and what I didn't. I let them see my uncertainty, but also my resolve. I talked about cash flow honestly. I shared decision points before they were made final. And I listened more than I spoke.

What I found was this: great leaders don't always have to inspire confidence by pretending to be certain. They inspire trust by being consistent. By showing up, again and again, with honesty, empathy, and clarity.

Reframing the Meaning of Legacy

For years, I had imagined that Luminations would be part of my family's legacy. I built it slowly, intentionally, with a sense of permanence. I thought perhaps one day my children would take the reins, or that it would become a multi-generational business.

But life has a way of unfolding differently than we plan.

As my children grew into their own careers—one in healthcare, one in education, another in speech therapy—I began to see that legacy was not about passing something down. It was about building something that could stand on its own. Something durable. Something values-based. Something that didn't require my name or presence to thrive.

That realization shifted my thinking. I began to ask different questions:

- Could Luminations thrive without me at the helm?

- Who could best carry it forward with care and excellence?

- Would our core values—empathy, flexibility, and unparalleled performance—continue to live on, even if the structure evolved?

These were not easy questions. But they were necessary ones. They pushed me to examine where my ego was tied up in the business and to ask whether letting go might actually be the ultimate act of leadership.

At the same time, the company itself was evolving. Despite the challenges of the pandemic, our team was not just surviving—we were innovating. One of our most meaningful breakthroughs had come in the form of FleXforce®.

From Innovation to Identity: The Rise of FleXforce®

FleXforce® began as a small, focused initiative—a way to support new mothers returning to the workforce on flexible terms. It emerged from my lived experience. I had watched talented women struggle to re-enter the corporate world after having babies, often forced to choose between professional growth and family care.

But what started as a niche solution quickly became something larger. It turns out that, not only did new moms need flexible, meaningful work but many of our clients needed well-trained, flexible talent as well. FleXforce® team members seamlessly filled openings where permanent hires hadn't yet been found, headed up innovation and new product launches, and took on day-to-day brand management roles.

We saw that the need for flexibility wasn't unique to new mothers. It applied to parents of children at all ages. It applied to caregivers in the sandwich generation (myself included). It was beneficial for professionals in transition: those pursuing advanced degrees, certifications, or new life chapters. FleXforce® became more than a staffing solution. It became a mission.

We began to match life stages with professional opportunities. We embraced non-linear paths. We provided part-time and flexible roles without sacrificing the standard of excellence our clients expected. We proved that flexible part-time talent could drive full-time growth and impact.

This model resonated with clients, not just because it was effective, but because it was human. It reflected a new reality—one in which people could bring their full selves to work. It showed that companies could adapt to people's lives, not just the other way around.

FleXforce® became the soul of Luminations. It was a living embodiment of our values in action. As our brand grew, so did our belief. Flexibility was not a perk. It was a phenomenal business strategy.

The Decision to Sell

In the midst of the pandemic, before the dust settled, acquisition conversations began to resurface. Unlike with earlier inquiries, this time I was ready to listen with a different mindset. I didn't view potential acquisition as a threat to what I had built. I saw it as a way to extend it.

However, I knew this couldn't be just any deal. It had to be the right deal—with the right people. So, I approached the process as I would any major strategic initiative: with intention, structure, and the right advisors.

I interviewed eight investment banks before choosing SLS Capital Advisors, a woman-led firm with both financial acumen and emotional intelligence. Stephanie Gaffin and her partner, Mark, brought a rare blend of rigor and respect. They didn't just run numbers, they took the time to understand our culture, our clients, our team and our process.

For legal representation, I turned to Karen Hermann at Venable, who was one of a small cadre of women in the country with deep expertise in M&A law. Karen navigated complex deal terms with precision and grace, preserving what mattered most: our people and our principles.

This was not just a financial exercise. It was an exercise in values-aligned leadership. I wanted to ensure that Luminations would land in hands that saw our people not as headcount, but as hearts and minds. I wanted partners who respected our model and understood the strategic potential of FleXforce®.

We approached the market with focus and care. I shared a curated list of over 50 potential Luminations acquirers that included former clients, friendly competitors, and partner firms. SLS expanded that list exponentially. From that broader pool, many responded but one company rose above the rest: The Market Performance Group (MPG).

MPG's founder, Marc Greenberger, and I had worked together at Johnson & Johnson. We shared a foundational respect for operational excellence, client impact, and top-tier talent. Many of their executives had once been my clients—people I trusted and admired. Marc treated his customers as friends and partners and always overdelivered. He and I saw client relationships in the same way. However, what truly sealed the deal was their reaction to FleXforce®.

They didn't see it as a novelty. They saw it as a strategic differentiator. That told me everything.

Leadership After the Sale

The sale of The Luminations Group to MPG was finalized on December 23, 2021. I stayed on as an executive, partly to ensure a smooth transition, and partly because I knew I wasn't done growing. Of course, my staying was also part of the deal – something that was important to me and to the acquiring company. I wanted to contribute. I also wanted to observe: how do two companies, with distinct strengths and histories, come together without compromising what makes each unique?

Integration was a leadership challenge of a different kind.

There were systems to merge, roles to redefine, and communications to align. But the real work was cultural. My role shifted from being the sole decision-maker to becoming part of a larger team. I was still leading business development, still sourcing top talent, still engaging with clients—but now within a new operating context.

It stretched me. It humbled me. It made me better.

MPG gave me space to grow. I taught part-time at Rutgers. I explored new projects. I found joy in mentoring younger professionals. The one year I had planned to stay turned into three.

Then, just as I had once known when to step in, I began to sense it was time to step aside.

Knowing When to Step Aside

I've come to believe that strong leaders need to know when to let go, not just when to lean in. As MPG scaled toward becoming a billion-dollar enterprise, the rhythm of the business began to shift. I found myself craving a return to the more intimate, entrepreneurial space where I had once thrived.

I had built Luminations to be agile, deeply human, and client immersed. As the organization expanded, I recognized that the group would benefit from new leadership, from someone equipped to systematize and to operationalize at a different level. With MPG's support, I handpicked and trained my successor, a former client and consultant. She stepped in and I stepped out.

So, just like that, the chapter closed.

Leadership Lessons to Carry Forward

Selling a business is a strategic milestone. It marks the culmination of years—sometimes decades—of vision, sacrifice, innovation, and grit. But for those who have walked that path, we know it's far more than a transactional event. It's a highly personal experience, one that calls on both our sharpest thinking and our deepest feeling. It requires intelligence and intuition. Determination and discernment. Strength and strategy and finally fortitude and flexibility.

In the process of letting go of the company I built, I discovered that true leadership—especially during transitions—isn't rooted in control. It's grounded in clarity which doesn't come from spreadsheets or strategic plans alone. It comes from being willing to pause, reflect, and choose your next step with intent. Exiting my business was more than a professional decision. It was a moment of transformation that unearthed profound truths about what leadership really means.

One of those truths is this: **leadership doesn't end with the exit**. In fact, it evolves. It becomes quieter, more internal, and at times, even more powerful. We often think of leadership as forward momentum, as action. Sometimes, the most courageous act of leadership is letting go—so that others can rise, so that culture can carry forward without you at the helm, and so that you, the leader, can become something new.

This understanding of leadership wasn't just shaped by boardrooms and business strategy. It was also shaped around kitchen tables and quiet phone calls with my mother, Arlene Burnett, who was one of my earliest and most beloved advisors. She had a gift for grounding me with wisdom that seemed simple on the surface but held layers of truth beneath.

There is one quote of hers that I return to often, especially in moments of transition:

"You don't have to know what you want to do when you grow up. You just need to know what you want to do next."

What a beautiful way to frame a life, a career, or a chapter of change. Her words reminded me that confidence doesn't always mean having a grand plan. Sometimes, it means trusting your instincts enough to take the next step, even if the whole path isn't visible yet.

As I stand now at the threshold of what comes next, I know that my journey isn't over; it's simply changing form. I now have the freedom—and the privilege—to explore new directions aligned with my evolving passions. Leadership, for me, is no longer just about growing a business. It's about growing myself. It's about mentoring others, sharing the lessons I've earned, and staying open to new possibilities.

One of the most important lessons I've learned, and perhaps the one I hope to carry forward into every future role is this:

Leadership is often simply the act of reminding others that it's going to be alright.

In times of uncertainty, people don't just look to their leaders for answers. They look to them for steadiness. Your team isn't just observing your decisions; they're studying your demeanor. How you show up in moments of ambiguity teaches more than any presentation ever could.

Because leadership is also defined by what we leave behind, I hope that what I left behind was more than a company. It was a belief system.

One that honored flexibility.
One that celebrated excellence.
One that made space for real lives and real growth.

So, as I move into this new season, I will take with me the lessons of clarity, of presence, of trust and my mother's wisdom – knowing that my next chapter doesn't need to be mapped out completely to be meaningful. Leadership isn't about always knowing what's next. It's about being willing to take the next step—with courage, humility, and grace even in uncertainty.

Leveraging Leadership Concepts – So What Now?

1. Build your business with an exit in mind, even if it feels far away. That doesn't make you disloyal. It makes you responsible.

2. Protect your culture during change. It's one of your most valuable, fragile, and transferable assets. Decide which elements of culture need to be preserved.

3. Talk to colleagues about choosing a buyer and transitioning through the exit process.

4. Stay long enough to ensure continuity. However, not so long that you hold back progress.

5. Work on identifying what you want to do next, but do not think you need to have a specific, executable plan from day one. Explore options, pick a direction and then take the first step.

REFERENCES

Chapter One:

- https://winstonchurchill.org/the-life-of-churchill/life/churchill-leader-and-statesman/

- https://www.fastcompany.com/90205427/doris-kearns-goodwin-knows-what-presidential-leadership-looks-like

- https://www.lifehack.org/articles/productivity/10-leadership-lessons-from-inspiring-leaders-history.html

- *Leadership in Turbulent Times* by Doris Kearns Goodwin

- *Churchill: A Life* by Sir Martin Gilbert

- *Sir Winston Churchill* by David Duke

- *Cleopatra: A Life* by Stacy Shiff

Chapter Two:

- https://www.businessnewsdaily.com/5537-how-to-be-ethical-leader.html

- https://www.forbes.com/sites/forbescoachescouncil/2018/08/06/11-ways-to-be-a-more-ethical-leader/#41ee8476cd48

- https://www.villanovau.com/resources/leadership/what-is-ethical-leadership/#.W-nDlOJN5PY

- https://ctb.ku.edu/en/table-of-contents/leadership/leadership-ideas/ethical-leadership/main

- *Culture Hacker* by Shane Green

Chapter Three:

- https://growingleaders.com/blog/passion-and-leadership/

- https://aboutleaders.com/leadership-skills-2-great-leaders-ignite-passion/#gs.SLvUhNI

- https://www.industryleadersmagazine.com/science-passionate-leadership-work/

- http://danblackonleadership.info/archives/1273

- https://aboutleaders.com/leadership-skills-2-great-leaders-ignite-passion/#gs.SLvUhNI

- https://takeitpersonelly.com/2013/10/14/5-reasons-why-vision-is-important-in-leadership/

- https://www.coadyperformance.group/coady-blog/2018/3/9/the-5-most-important-reasons-why-great-leadership-is-vital

Chapter Four:

- https://www.forbes.com/sites/sunniegiles/2018/05/09/how-vuca-is-reshaping-the-business-environment-and-what-it-means-for-innovation/#205bd997eb8d

- https://drjohnsullivan.com/uncategorized/vuca-the-new-normal-for-talent-management-and-workforce-planning/

Chapter Five:

- https://www.forbes.com/sites/patrickhull/2013/01/28/3-steps-to-build-the-right-team/#1e85cf1a36b8

- https://www.oreilly.com/business/free/files/learning-how-to-delegate-as-a-leader.pdf

- https://www.wikihow.com/Build-a-Good-Team-for-Business-Success

- Start-Up Nation: The Story of Israel's Economic Miracle by Dan Senor and Saul Singer

Chapter Six:

- *Speak Up, Show Up and Stand Out* by Dr. Loretta Malandro

- https://www.forbes.com/sites/mikemyatt/2012/04/04/10-communication-secrets-of-great-leaders/#440065ac22fe

Chapter Seven:

- "Leader" by Joseph Folkman

- *The Quit Alternative* by Ben Fanning

- https://www.inc.com/ben-fanning/7-ways-top-leaders-develop-grit-in-their-team.html

- https://www.amazon.com/Alive-Work-Neuroscience-Helping-People/dp/1633694259

- https://www.ted.com/talks/angela_lee_duckworth_grit_the_power_of_passion_and_perseverance?language=en

- *Learning to Delegate as a Leader* by Esther Schindler

- *Alive at Work: The Neuroscience of Helping People Love What They Do* by Daniel Cable

Chapter Eight:

- https://www.elle.com/culture/career-politics/advice/a27473/aggressive-or-assertive-bitchy-or-blunt-3-women-on-overcoming-sexist-feedback-at-workand-rising-up-through-the-ranks/

- https://www.forbes.com/sites/forbescoachescouncil/2018/02/26/15-biggest-challenges-women-leaders-face-and-how-to-overcome-them/#2b39af584162

- https://shecancode.io/blog/role-models-are-key-in-gender-diversity-especially-in-tech-engineering

- https://www.sciencedirect.com/science/article/pii/S0022103113000206

- https://eccles.utah.edu/news/breaking-glass-ceiling-3-career-strategies-women/

- https://www.leadership-central.com/challenges-of-women-in-leadership-roles.html

- https://www.washingtonpost.com/business/2018/09/24/pew-survey-women-fare-better-most-leadership-traits/?noredirect=on&utm_term=.a7e54f7862e0

Chapter Nine:

- https://www.routledge.com/Good-Leaders-Learn-Lessons-from-Lifetimes-of-Leadership-1st-Edition/Seijts/p/book/9780415659772

- https://www.td.org/insights/leadership-cant-be-taught-but-it-can-be-learned

Chapter Ten:

- https://www.virgin.com/branson-family/richard-branson-blog/introducing-my-class-on-masterclass